# HE HOPED I WOULD COME

*A DYING FATHER'S WISH*

SUSIE KEEFER

SECANT PUBLISHING
SALISBURY, MARYLAND

HE HOPED I WOULD COME:
A Dying Father's Wish
Copyright © 2024 by Susie Keefer

All Rights Reserved. No part of this publication may be reproduced, distributed or transmitted in any form or by any means, including photocopying, recording, or other electronic or mechanical methods, without the prior written permission of the publisher or author, except in the case of brief quotations embodied in critical reviews and certain other non-commercial uses permitted by copyright law.

Scripture quotations taken from The Holy Bible, New International Version® NIV®. Copyright © 1973, 1978, 1984, 2011 by Biblica, Inc. Used with permission. All rights reserved worldwide.

Secant Publishing, LLC
615 North Pinehurst Avenue
Salisbury MD 21801
www.secantpublishing.com

ISBN 979-8-9903562-0-7 (hardcover)
ISBN 979-8-9886410-9-4 (paperback)
ISBN 979-8-9903562-1-4 (ebook)

Library of Congress Control Number: 2024905785

To Ed, my husband and best friend
Who has always been the wind beneath my wings
I love you

# Contents

| | |
|---|---|
| Foreword | vii |
| Introduction | 1 |
| Chapter 1: Here I Am, Lord… Maybe | 3 |
| Chapter 2: Locked Up Abroad…Almost | 15 |
| Chapter 3: DRC … A Humanitarian Crisis | 21 |
| Chapter 4: Encircled…Overcoming Fear with Joy | 25 |
| Chapter 5: Meeting Jubilee…Joy and Realization | 33 |
| Chapter 6: The Congo River…Peaceful | 39 |
| Chapter 7: An Unexpected Connection…A Promise to Keep | 45 |
| Chapter 8: The Sending Party…A Piece of My Heart | 51 |
| Chapter 9: Time to Go…Melancholy Blues | 57 |
| Chapter 10: From the Mountains…To the Equator | 61 |
| Chapter 11: Return…Expand | 65 |
| Chapter 12: Unexpected…Perfect | 75 |
| Chapter 13: Family…A New Definition | 83 |
| Chapter 14: Reassurance…And That Promise | 91 |
| Chapter 15: Hurry Up…And Wait | 99 |
| Chapter 16: Heartbreak…Blessings Overflowing | 109 |
| Chapter 17: Questions…Answers | 121 |

| | |
|---|---:|
| Chapter 18: Faith Is a Noun…Trust Is a Verb | 127 |
| Afterword (Miriam Oleka Keefer) | 131 |
| Acknowledgments | 133 |
| About the Author | 135 |
| For Further Reading | 137 |

# Foreword

THERE IS NOTHING more precious in a person's life than discovering a social environment that is distinctly different from their accustomed environment, and choosing to come and live in that new environment—which may be totally different in culture, in social interactions, in food, and in housing. Taking that leap requires a high degree of spirituality and faith. To reach this level and make this vision a reality, several factors must be present in a person that we can only call *passion* for others.

I am the Mission Coordinator for the Central Congo United Methodist Episcopal Area. I work as a liaison for the Peter D. Weaver Congo Partnership, coordinating the efforts of our U.S. Partners and our Congolese program directors and staff. I met Susie Keefer for the first time in August of 2010, when she arrived with a small team representing the U.S. Partners. Over the past thirteen years, Susie's love for the Congolese people has brought her to become part of our family.

This book allows the reader to walk with Susie through her passionate adventure, which was not without risk, allowing us to smell, taste, hear, see, and feel every detail of her encounters. She has become known as a mother of many children, demonstrating to the Congolese community the true face of a Christian who lives for the betterment of others.

Indeed, during these thirteen years of visiting the Congo, Susie has been remarkable not only in her interaction with many children, but also with the elderly, and even the destitute. The people are always surprised at her affection for embracing them. The area in which she is closely involved is called Mpasa I. It was settled with refugees from war-torn areas arriving with nothing to build a new life. It became known as the land of the forsaken.

Each of Susie's visits is an opportunity for inspiration in the activities of the partnership. She works for the health of vulnerable people whom she has never ceased to dialogue with, touch, cuddle, and hold in a loving way without discrimination. Her integration into Congolese social life has shown all of us that through faith, there are no differences of race or skin color (black or white, yellow or red). Even her American compatriots found in her a real model for how to live harmoniously with the Congolese.

In this book, Susie presents a rare event related to the adoption of a little girl called Miriam, whom she met at the nutrition center during her second visit to Congo in 2011. The adoption of Miriam is a very exceptional testimony. In fact, Miriam, a little girl abandoned by her mother, will win the affection she lost by appealing to the maternal instinct of a stranger.

*He Hoped I Would Come* is a product of a reality lived in Congo. Miriam has made Congolese history. Thanks to her and Susie's passion, a nutritional center in her honor was created called Miriam's Table, feeding 350 children a day and offering a future of health and well-being to the Congolese people. This book tells that story from its beginning to the current day, with a future that is still unfolding. God's plan is unfathomable.

*Dr. Adolphe Yamba Yamba Lukavu*
*Mission Coordinator for the Central Congo Episcopal Area*
*Surgeon with Specialty in Mother and Child Health*

# Introduction

*However, as it is written:*
*"What no eye has seen,*
*what no ear has heard,*
*and what no human mind has conceived"—*
*the things God has prepared for those who love him—*

1 CORINTHIANS 2:9

A S I WALK through this journey called life, I look back and smile to myself as I see how beautifully God has been orchestrating even the smallest details. As I was living each day, I was never really thinking about it, but hindsight brings a noticeably clear picture. Who knew that the seventeen years I spent leading youth mission teams into the Appalachian Mountains each summer was a training ground for what He planned for me in the future? As I moved from those lush green mountains to the sweltering heat of the African equator… an orphaned child and a ministry awaited.

Come with me as I chronicle for you my personal walk with God. As in all our lives, there are times of boundless joy and times of heartbreak, but all along the path, we see God's hand reaching down and pulling us through. Sometimes, we need to curl up in His lap and weep, other times dance with joy before His throne, but most often we need to kneel quietly at His feet and listen for His grace-filled whisper in our ears.

CHAPTER 1

# Here I Am, Lord... Maybe

*Then I heard the voice of the Lord, saying, "Whom shall I send? And who will go for us?" Then I said, "Here am I. Send me!"*

ISAIAH 6:8

AS A YOUNG girl, paging through my mother's magazines, I paused to stare at a haunting picture of a boy with eyes like dark pools of murky brown water. He sat among rubbish with a basketball-sized belly appended with sticklike arms and legs. I felt a lump in my throat and tears welled in my eyes. My heart sensed a sadness that, at the time, was beyond my understanding. I realized much later that I was looking at an advertisement to save the starving children in Biafra who were affected by a raging war with Nigeria.

Fast forward now to 2010, when the vehicle I am riding in is crawling through rutted sandy roads. Looking through the open window, that haunting picture is staring back at me; only this time it is real life. I am in the Democratic Republic of the Congo.

I was just ten years old when I came upon that picture of the severely malnourished little boy, but I never forgot him or others that I continued to see in the magazines. The desolation in their eyes had pierced my soul.

During my junior high school years, each summer I spent a week at Cherry Run Camp, a United Methodist Church camp nestled in the hills of Clarion County, Pennsylvania. The camp's primary mission then and now is "to make disciples of Jesus Christ, and to encourage believers to advance in their faith." Although I did not go there with the intention of deepening my faith, it was during those weeks of camp that God began to work in my heart.

At that time, Cherry Run was a 75-year-old camp made up of family homes converted into camp housing. Heavy wooden bunk beds replaced Victorian beds with matching dressers, and handmade quilts. The bathrooms had been remodeled to withstand much heavier traffic too. Most of the big front porches remained, perfect for evening gatherings before a short walk to the camp snack shop, our nightly routine after evening service. Some of the other homes scattered throughout were still owned by families that had been attending the camp meeting for generations.

Evening services were held in a large worship pavilion with long white wooden benches that descended to the pulpit area with a grand choir loft behind. After dinner, we would change into dresses, the required female attire, while the boys added a dress shirt and tie. The choir loft was filled with adult choir members singing in rehearsed four-part harmony. It was the pinnacle for each camp day, but it was not the high point that my friends and I were particularly anxious to reach. That high point came after the service, when we had a chance to see the boys we had crushes on. We were hoping for a walk with them around the big circle driveway. If we were lucky, we might even hold hands!

The summer I was fourteen, the featured speaker was a missionary living and working in a developing country. He was sharing his calling with aspirations of touching the hearts of our camp full of young people to follow Christ into the mission field. Most of the time my mind was wandering or figuring out ways to sign to my friends, as no talking was permitted (adults were posted throughout to be sure that rule was followed). An occasional stern look made us sit up a little straighter and at least pretend to be listening. One evening, like a dial being changed on a radio, my mind drifted back from distant thoughts to tune in to what was being said. In the speaker's final words, his appeal was for those who felt God was calling them into the mission field.

As he asked for those who heard that call to come forward, I felt a gentle pulling, like an invisible thread, to step out, leave my friends behind, and walk down as he continued to pray. Though numerous others were standing along with me, I sensed an aloneness with God speaking only to me—no details, just a call to commitment. I had no idea what this commitment entailed, but a desire to serve was planted in my heart that evening. That moment became the root of the path my life was to take.

IT WAS IN LATE August of 2010 when I arrived at the N'djili airport in Kinshasa, the capital city of the Democratic Republic of the Congo. It was about six in the evening. Surprisingly, darkness had already set in. As the plane door opened, I was struck by intense heat, not even a feather breath of coolness. As I descended the steps, I saw that everyone ahead of me was being herded into a standing-room-only bus. Upon hitting the ground, I was also stuffed into it. When the door closed, the air inside was so stifling, it was like breathing steam from a hot cup of tea.

I had been traveling for over twenty-seven hours. Weariness did not begin to describe how I was feeling physically, but somehow my senses were on overdrive, keeping my body in motion, and my emotions on high alert. As I stood there on the moving bus, my body slightly swaying, sweat dripping, and seeing nothing even slightly familiar, apprehension set in. One thought was taking stage front... "What have I done?"

Had God really asked me to come here? Was I sure it was His voice I had heard?

As the bus pulled up to the terminal, I peered through the window, seeing a small, dimly lit airport. As we got closer my eyes widened and my body stiffened as panic began to crawl through me. Everywhere I looked I saw uniformed soldiers and police all carrying machine guns over their shoulders. Honestly, at this point, I was hoping to stay on the bus, despite the smelly, sweltering heat.

Nevertheless, we were immediately ushered inside to a small room. As we were in the bus, we continued to be jammed together in a room too small for an airplane full of people. It was old and austere like a courthouse, with rich mahogany booths on the far end where several customs officers sat. My uneasiness kept me from looking around too much for fear of making eye contact with the soldiers, but soon enough, curiosity won out. As I gazed around, I saw that not a single Congolese face was welcoming us to their country. Here I stood, drained from the long travel, laden with paperwork and carry-ons, realizing with trepidation that I would be here for ten days. My confidence that God brought me here continued to gradually dissolve.

Slowly, the guards started to move us on through the line. When it was my turn to step up to the customs window, a stern-looking, gruff-voiced man started asking me questions... in French. As I needed to stand on my tiptoes to see and hear him, I flushed with fright, as he got more perturbed that I was unable to answer his questions. White, English-speaking Americans must come in limited numbers, because as I looked around that crowded room, I realized that I and the other three team members were the only ones.

I do not remember how I made it beyond that customs officer to the other side, but through the crush of unsmiling faces, directly ahead of me, like sunlight peeking through dark clouds, I saw one incredibly beautiful smile. Beaming with happiness that we had safely arrived, stood Adolphe Yamba Yamba, our Mission Coordinator. His smile washed a calmness over me. I did not know it then, but this smiling man would come to play a significant role in the lives of me and my family.

With confidence, Adolphe shuffled us through the crowd to a small waiting room, which for the first time since our arrival was not brimming with people, but instead offered soft seating and air conditioning. As I began to sit down, I felt my body melt and flow onto that seat like warm honey as my angst started to drip slowly away.

Leaving the airport, we drove slowly through the congested capital city of Kinshasa. I remembered from our team preparations that this city was built for about four million people but there were now over eight million living here, so the masses were forced to devise ways to cope. Through the struggles of their overladen, poverty-stricken lives, there emerged two groups of people—night people and day people. The day people share a home of sorts with the night people, trading places from working to sleeping quarters and back again.

Even though the night was well upon us, the streets were crowded with Mardi Gras-like noise and music. As I watched the city pass by through the open car windows, my nostrils burned and my eyes began to tear from the pungent smell of smoldering garbage piled along the streets. But it was the commotion from the myriad of night people beginning their "day" that held my attention. Hundreds of vendors lined the streets behind small tables with umbrellas and burning candles, selling wares ranging from cell phone minutes to fresh ground flour for bread. The streets were as busy as if the sun were shining instead of the moon. There was a cacophony of booming music, loud laughing voices, and blaring horns among the congestion of people and vehicles trying to squeeze their way through to their destinations.

There were no driving rules, no lights or road signs. It appeared that every driver was blowing his horn while pedestrians pushed their way through the maze of gridlocked cars. I sat there staring out the window in astonishment at these resilient people.

We continued to inch our way through the tangle to our guesthouse, about twenty-five kilometers from the airport. Not knowing what our accommodations would be like, I was pleasantly surprised to be greeted by a lovely American couple surrounded by a large gathering area with subtle African décor. Off to the side were long dining tables covered with African print tablecloths, one catching my eye. Upon it awaited our dinner—American-style pizza with salad and a sweet dessert. At the table was our fifth team member, Karen Morgan. She had been part of a previous team but remained at the guest house to help guide our team. She too was a bright spot in this foreign place. We had met during our team planning sessions.

As we sat around the table together, I was most taken by her love for the Congolese people and the importance of being respectful to their cultural traditions, not trying to thoughtlessly push our American habits on them. I felt a kinship to her and wanted to emulate her respect and love for a people I had yet to meet.

With more than thirty hours of travel, I was ready to sleep. However, the world around us was pulsing with sound. Across the road in front of our charming guest house was a nightclub, bursting with people and blaring music. Behind us was a different source of booming music, accompanied by a thundering voiced preacher, who could be heard easily over the competing blasts of music. Somehow, through the thumping of the bass sounds and the roaring of the preacher, exhaustion overtook me. I fell asleep, enveloped in the sounds of Kinshasa, all the time wondering how this unbelievable journey would be woven into the tapestry the Master Weaver was weaving for me.

In her book, *The Hiding Place*, Corrie Ten Boom writes:

> Occasionally God gives us a glimpse at what He is weaving into the fabric of our lives. That momentary peek at glory gives us the courage to soldier on, knowing that nothing happens by accident.

Our lives are like tapestries magnificently filled with color and intricate details. Tapestry weaving is an extremely labor-intensive process creating extraordinary pieces of art. It is a form of textile art, traditionally woven by hand on a loom. The vertical threads are known as warps, and the horizontal threads are known as wefts. The vertical warp threads are vital components of each piece—they are the backbone of every tapestry and provide the support for the weft threads. All the warp threads are hidden in the completed work, creating an aesthetically pleasing piece of art. This is different from balanced weaves, where both the warp and weft appear equally in the fabric. God takes the "weft" threads of our lives—the parts where we have lost our focus on Him, straying from the path He has planned. Where our weft threads have caused confusion and angst for us, He uses them to build strength and character, weaving them among His "warp" threads creating that richness of Him within us. I knew even then that in His time, He would let me see how this African journey would become part of the life tapestry He was and is still designing for me.

WITH THE SUNLIGHT OF a new day shining in, I awoke incredibly early. My head was still in another time zone. I remembered it was Sunday and we would be meeting Adolphe for worship. Butterflies fluttered in my stomach as I felt mixed emotions of delight and curiosity, wondering what a Congolese worship service would be like.

Since it was still quite early and breakfast would not be served for a couple more hours, I decided to explore MPH, our home away from home for the next ten days. MPH stands for Methodist Presbyterian Hostel. I learned that in the late 1960s, there were many missionaries in Congo with various mission organizations. When The American School of Kinshasa (TASOK) was started, missionaries around the country needed to find a way to board their children so they could attend the school here in Kinshasa. Every mission had its hostels with its own hostel parents: Mennonites, Baptists, Christian and Missionary Alliance, Disciples of Christ, Methodists, and Presbyterians, to name a few.

The Methodist and Presbyterian missionaries got together, obtained the land, and built this building. It was designed to hold about eighty children, and two sets of hostel parents, complete with kitchen, laundry, dining room, library, music rooms, and garage. It is set on several acres of land, right across the street from the American School.

MPH is the only Protestant-run guesthouse left in Kinshasa. There are many hotels and places called guest houses, but none of them have the "oasis" feel that MPH gives. Clay and Cindy Dunn became the managers in 2010. Since then, they have overseen many projects, Clay doing most of the work himself, updating the facility with more modern touches, at the same time, keeping the feel of the history it holds.

Upon our arrival, each of our names was printed on a chalk board welcoming us. We knew the food would be safe to eat with filtered water to drink. We had a computer with internet, electricity, hot water for showers and even a library filled with books of every genre for guests to enjoy during their stay! An oasis is defined as a fertile or green spot in the desert representing a type of shelter from the storm. It is a moment of respite from the conditions of the desert. Over the next ten days, MPH would prove to be that place of respite for us. A place for us to gather and talk about our experiences for the day—what struck our hearts, what lifted us, or what brought sadness or despair. A place for nourishment. A place for rest. A true oasis.

Marie was the leader of our five-member team. She had not been to Congo before but had led several mission trips to other foreign countries. Wes, our only male member, had been to Congo six years earlier with a small team. As we traveled each day, he found that many things had changed, especially newly paved roads still under construction, causing some difficulty in travel. Karen, whom I mentioned we met up with our first night at MPH, had been to Congo in 2002 and again in 2004. Her trip in 2004 included flying further into the Upcountry with a small team chosen by the current Bishop. Her knowledge of Congolese culture and her fresh experiences in the past fifteen days proved to be extremely beneficial as we navigated through our days together. Tika was the fifth and youngest member of our team, also on her first African experience. We each came from different churches, with different experiences in missions, but for this trip we came sharing one heart: to engulf ourselves in the culture of the Congolese people and bring these experiences home to raise awareness of the needs of our ministries there.

As a team, we were representing the Peter D. Weaver Congo Partnership, a ministry a United Methodist bishop had started by answering a cry for help. The Congo Partnership had its beginnings in the late 1990s through a denominational initiative called Hope for the Children of Africa. In response to a request from African bishops in the United Methodist Church (UMC), a task force was created to assist in providing relief and reconciliation to innocent children who had been victims of wars, famines, and the destruction of schools and hospitals.

Every U.S. Annual Conference in the UMC was asked to partner with an African country or episcopal area. In early 2000, Peter D. Weaver, resident bishop of the Peninsula-Delaware Conference, and other conference leaders saw that no other conference in the U.S. had chosen Central Congo. Through prayer, discernment, and consensus, the Peninsula-Delaware Conference agreed to partner with the Central Congo Episcopal Area under the leadership of Bishop Joseph Fama Onema. Immediate financial support for the construction of an orphanage outside Kinshasa began and, in 2001, the Congo Partnership was officially launched. It began support of the Mpasa Medical & Nutrition Center in a refugee area outside Kinshasa which had been initiated by UMCOR (United Methodist Committee on Relief) during the refugee crisis in the late 1990s, when refugees fled to Congo from South Sudan, Angola, and east Congo. All the Democratic Republic of Congo was engaged in civil conflict, making the initial years of the Partnership challenging.

But God continued to provide, allowing the U.S. partners to travel to Congo in 2002 and again in 2004, as the conflict ceased. To honor Bishop Weaver and his vision, the program was named the Peter D. Weaver Congo Partnership in 2004.

With the goal of self-sustainability for all projects, the Congolese are responsible for providing leadership and overseeing what is necessary for their success. The scope of the projects in Congo grew to include various medical centers, schools, farm projects, nutrition projects, children's ministry, freshwater wells, and cataract treatment missions.

THAT FIRST MORNING, A lovely Congolese staff, whom Clay and Cindy trained to cook American food, served our breakfast. It was obvious they felt honored to be part of the MPH ministry. While eating breakfast together, Clay and Cindy shared how they had spent months teaching them how to cook popular American food dishes. It was not an easy task as most of the food, as well as many of the ingredients, were foreign to them. Now, they served them with pride and were enjoying eating some of them too—especially the sweets, like brownies. The Dunns had created an MPH family that delighted in pleasing the guests.

Once we finished eating, we gathered our things for travel and headed to the car. For safety, MPH is gated with high cement walls around the property, so cars must wait for a staff member to open it to enter and exit. Each time, a short toot of the horn would bring someone running. Our driver was a small older man introduced to us as "Papa." He did not know or understand English, and we did not speak the local language of Lingala or French, but he managed quite well getting us to the church to meet Adolphe.

As we neared the church, our car slowed to a crawl with the narrowing roads. With our windows already down from the early morning heat, I noticed our vehicle, filled with white people, triggered a vast number of stares from the people walking along the sides of the roads. As I waved with a smile, some of the children looked with both wide-eyed curiosity and angst at never seeing a white-skinned person before, let alone a carful. Some waved back, but we kept hearing *mindeli* being shouted from some in the crowds. We later found out it means "white person" in Lingala. Gazing ahead of us, I recognized Adolphe arriving on the back of a motorcycle, still wearing that infectious smile.

Our host church, the Mabondeli United Methodist Church, was nestled back from the road, standing taller than the surrounding buildings as if it were calling out to the passersby to come in and see what it was all about. As we began to move with the flow of people toward the building, we could hear the worship music drifting through the air.

Approaching the opened doors, I was moved by the smiling faces awaiting our arrival. After a quick greeting, we were led to the front of the church where a row of white plastic chairs awaited us across the front. I knew then that we must be considered special guests because the rest of the congregation were seated on rows of straight wooden benches.

Surprisingly, the building had electricity, allowing it to be equipped with a sound system. After falling asleep to the mega sound system from the night before, I was not surprised at the volume supplied this morning.

Adolphe was translating for us throughout the service. I needed to concentrate fully on his words to understand what was being said. At one point in the service, our team was invited to come up and share about who we were and our purpose for being in Congo. As I stood there facing the large crowd of worshippers, I saw a glow of pride among them. The pride of worship. The pride of knowing that their praise is heard. The pride of sharing their place of worship with strangers from half a world away.

The praise and worship were like a hot air balloon filled to the brim, allowing it to float through the sky bursting with color. There were different choirs of children, youth, men, and women with synchronized dancing. Some were wearing matching fabric outfits. The fabrics with such bright bold colors seemed to enhance the glory of the adoration. The clock was never watched. There was no planned time to close worship. No one, not even the pastor, was watching the time or seemed anxious to leave.

The giving of tithes and offerings was a grand time of honor. No plate was passed in these worship services. Everyone came forward to place their offering in a basket. There were three labeled baskets on the offering table—one for ladies, one for men, and one for youth. The ladies were dressed in their finest Congolese dresses with ruffles, sashes, and color, making even a rainbow seem plain. As they moved toward the baskets, they danced a traditional dance with faces raised up and glowing. I was mesmerized by the beauty of it as they placed their rolled-up bills in the basket and continued around the room, dancing with gratefulness.

When the celebration of worship was complete, the service ended. We were gathered and led to a small room at the back of the church building. Bottles of soda, bananas, and peanuts were served. Gathered with us were the leaders of the church. Since no one in our group spoke French or Lingala, we depended on Adolphe to keep our conversation going. Right here, in this small, crowded room, the feeling of anxiety of making a mistake in coming to this foreign place was slowly dissolving as I felt a thread of connection being woven between these people and me.

CHAPTER 2

# Locked Up Abroad… Almost

*I sought the LORD, and he answered me;
he delivered me from all my fears.*

PSALM 34:4

AS WE LEFT MPH Monday morning, Papa tooted the horn for the gate to open. Off we went to meet Adolphe and travelled on to the Mpasa Medical and Nutrition Center, our first adventure through the city in daylight. With our worship experience from Sunday morning still on my mind, I was feeling exhilarated to see what this day had in store for us.

Upon our arrival, Adolphe had explained that tourist cameras were not welcome in the streets of Kinshasa—particularly in a vehicle full of white faces, which stood out like a beacon. We had to be very mindful not to cause offense by raising our cameras and snapping pictures. As we twisted our way down to where the roads began to be filled with crowds of people walking, obeying that directive became more difficult as picturesque scenes unfolded before us.

The streets were overflowing with a rainbow of bold-colored fabrics. Women were walking with large baskets balanced on their heads, filled with big green leafy vegetables, fresh pineapples, bananas, and even live caterpillars. Others shouting *mai, mai* (water in Lingala) carried large trays piled high with plastic bags filled with water. Some goods were neatly piled along the street with women and children stooped beside them, ready for a sale—peanuts, dried fish, clothing, car parts, and used books, to name a few that caught my eye. It seemed like everyone was selling something, calling out to passersby.

Passengers in cars were greeted with sellers holding their wares to the windows as they curled their way through the stalled lines of cars trapped in traffic jams. I was startled by the number of young boys weaving through the cars, particularly those selling sodas piled high in plastic bags on their heads. The weight they were carrying was inconceivable. Like a dance, they would gently lift the bag from their head, lower it to the ground, reach in for the chosen drink by the motorist, with that same hand take the money, and with one big sweep it would be back up on top of their head and off they would go.

Another captivating sight was those carrying dozens of hard-boiled eggs in cardboard trays piled ten to twelve trays high. For each sale, they too would slowly lower the pile down to the ground, peel the egg, place some mustard on it and hand it to the customer. Then they would return the stack of trays to the top of their heads. More food items, both packaged and fresh, maps, watches, passport covers, tissues, and even men's suits were available for sale. Other vendors stood among the cars like scarecrows, holding their arms straight out, with phone cords, belts, and a plethora of other items dangling.

It was an ant colony of busyness. Watching ants scurrying around on the ground shows no sense of order, but they live and work together in a highly organized society. Most ant colonies are so united toward the common purposes of survival and growth that they behave like a single organism. Day after day, I observed these sellers to have their own ant colony-like behaviors united to survive.

Still mesmerized by the dance of the sellers, we made our way slowly to a roundabout crowded with cars and soldiers. We were moving in snail-like fashion when one soldier stepped in front of us, halting our car. Papa tried to keep moving and blowing his horn, but this soldier was not budging.

Then, looking directly at Marie in the front passenger side, he came around to her side of the car. In a loud, almost shouting, voice, he asked her to get out of the car, which she refused. He tried to grab her arm and she pulled away. She reached down at her feet and got all our paperwork out to show who we were and our purpose for being in Congo. As foreigners, it was necessary that we carry our passports and the letters of invitation that were required for our visas to enter the country. He read them, but still did not seem satisfied to let us go on our way.

He then started toward the driver's side. As he moved away from the car, Papa tried to ignore him and started to move us forward, which was impossible with the multitude of cars. For a seemingly old man he was quite feisty. Without hesitation, another soldier stepped in front of the car, continuing our captivity in the crowd. Now both soldiers started yelling at Papa and eventually he produced his license. As we stared in disbelief, Karen told us to stay quiet, as any type of interference could cause more heightened reactions. With the soldiers' voices so loud and commanding, that was not a problem for me. I was so paralyzed with fear that no words could come out! At that moment, I was glad to be sitting far in the back in a fold-up seat, helping me to feel somewhat removed. Papa continued to be argumentative but seemed to be cooperating. For whatever reason, this did not satisfy either of the soldiers.

After looking at his license, they opened his door, demanding he get out of the car. He refused. The first soldier reached inside and grabbed the keys out of the ignition, while at the same time the other soldier was yanking Papa out of the car. He dragged him around to the back, opened the door where I was sitting, and shoved Papa in with me. Then, to my disbelief, he proceeded to squeeze in himself, while the other soldier jumped into the driver's seat, pressing us on through the vehicle-filled streets. Panic raced through me like a gunshot. What was happening? Where were we going? How would anyone know how to find us? Were we going to jail?

In silence we rode with the two soldiers in charge of our destination. It seemed eternal not knowing where we were going. With the soldier pressed up against me, now I was wishing I were in the front seat. I was sure he could feel my heart pounding like a drum.

We kept driving until we came to a place enclosed with a 10-foot-high, royal blue aluminum fence, topped with rolls of barbed wire. As we turned toward the gate, the soldier blew the horn, the gate was opened, and we drove in. Upon entering, my eyes widened as I saw many soldiers milling around, each with a gun strapped over his shoulder. My heart pounded even harder, as my breath caught, and dread crawled up my spine.

Karen, who had a lovely calming effect on others, opened her bag and pulled out a phone. It had been left with her by the leader of her prior team. It had service only in Congo and was intended to be used only to contact Adolphe for emergencies. This was an emergency! With the state the soldiers had been in prior to now, pulling out a phone may have only angered them more. Holding it up for the soldier to see, she motioned a questioning look asking to make a call. He approved it and she dialed Adolphe. Oddly, the soldier remained in the car bunched up against me. Between the heat of the day setting in and my heightened nerves, sweat was dripping down my back.

Adolphe answered quickly as he was already waiting for us at our agreed-upon meeting place. Karen gave him the details of our situation. He asked to talk directly to the soldier. The soldier continued talking in a booming authoritative voice. Not having an idea what was being said, we remained quiet and still. Finally, he handed the phone to Karen. Adolphe explained to her that arrests like these were often made to foreigners, as the soldiers saw it as an easy way to get money. He told us to give the soldier $50 and then we could be on our way.

At that moment, like the mist of a cool spring shower, relief washed over all of us, knowing that we were not going to be jailed. Adolphe later told us that the soldier originally had asked for $200—$50 from each of us—but he negotiated to $50 for the lot. When we found Adolphe waiting along the crowded street outside, he was smiling, bringing peace to my being once again.

He was not shocked at what had happened but felt quite badly that he had not met us directly at the guesthouse. From this day forward, he would be sure to come to meet us there for travel. This turned out to be a particularly good decision as the next day we were stopped once again. Luckily, Adolphe chose to wear his official United Methodist shirt with all our paperwork in hand. He crawled out from the back seat to talk with the soldier. He was an excellent negotiator as we were left to go on our way with no payoff needed. His next decision for travel was that he should ride in front with our driver so that the soldiers would not notice our car as easily with all our white faces.

Traveling through the city was difficult with traffic, but once we were on the outskirts, we moved swiftly along the newly built highway. The scenery was changing from crowded streets to trees and slightly more greenery. It was the dry season, so not as lush as the rainy season. The area we were going to was called the Mpasa I Region. When we turned off the highway, the road became nothing more than sandy dirt. Papa slowed to a near stop as he changed to four-wheel drive.

As I mentioned earlier, this area had been settled by refugees from other warring countries as well as thousands of Congolese from the eastern side of Congo. They fled ongoing wars with tribes from Uganda and Rwanda, and also from the Angolan war. The influx of so many refugees with few or no life-sustaining supplies had a devastating effect in an area already facing hunger.

As our driver continued inching through the uneven sandy path, I stared through the open window into this unknown world. I saw tiny houses built with dirty, gray-colored bricks that blended with the same dirty gray soil they sat on. The grass was sparse and mostly brown from the lack of rain and the scorching heat from the sun. Most every home had a brightly colored curtain for a door. Pieces of fabric and clothing lay randomly on nearby bushes or hung on a small piece of rope tied between trees to dry, offering splashes of color to the pallid bricks and soil. Groups of children sat playing in that dusty soil looking back at me, evoking that memory of those large sorrowful eyes, those swollen bellies, and those sticklike arms that stunned me so many years ago. I felt a familiar lump in my throat while my eyes filled with tears.

As we continued toward the Mpasa Medical Clinic and Nutrition Center, I was a little fearful about what my reactions would be once we arrived. I worried if I was going to be able to pull myself out of this bleak sadness I was experiencing and be able to put on a smile to meet and greet the staff and the children.

Since I had no visual description of the clinic and had not seen any pictures, I had no idea of what to expect in the way of buildings or staff. With the poverty-stricken existence I had seen thus far, I was not feeling optimistic. But as we rounded the final bend, to my surprise, sat a set of bright pink buildings. Our driver tooted the horn as we entered the driveway. Children and adults came running to greet us from all directions, stirring up quite a cloud of dust in that dry gray soil. Their smiles were bursting with joy and elation. Those fears I had slowly faded as their joy flowed around me like a soft blanket. I was going to be okay.

CHAPTER 3

# DRC ... A Humanitarian Crisis

*I remain confident of this: I will see the goodness of the* Lord
*in the land of the living. Wait for the* Lord*; be strong
and take heart and wait for the* Lord.

PSALMS 27:13-14

BEING INVITED TO join a mission team to travel to Africa, to a country I knew nothing about, was a big step. My only experiences outside of the USA had been related to our family business, traveling to Italy, Canada, Jamaica, and Grand Bahama Island. I knew nothing about the Democratic Republic of the Congo or what we hoped to accomplish there.

Once I joined the team, we met together several times to learn about the purpose of the trip, expectations, the cultural differences we would encounter, along with the history of the country and its severe poverty.

The Democratic Republic of the Congo (DRC) is located on the western side of central Africa with twenty-five miles of coastline. It is the second largest country in Africa, a little less than one-fourth the size of the USA. It is among the five poorest countries in the world and has struggled for decades with conflicts and vulnerability.

The DRC is one of the world's richest countries in terms of its vast natural resources, including copper, cobalt, and diamonds. But its people are some of the world's poorest, according to the UN Environmental Programme. In 2018, about 70 percent were subsisting on less than $1.90 a day. Added to this widespread poverty are ongoing political conflicts and food shortages. Raising a family, to say the least, is extremely difficult in these conditions.

One interesting fact I found, offering hope that our team would be welcomed by many, is that a large majority of the population is Christian. Estimates vary, but *Encyclopedia Britannica* says 50 percent are Roman Catholic, 20 percent Protestant, and 10 percent indigenous Christian. Traditional religions are also widely practiced.

To learn more about the country's history, I was given the book *King Leopold's Ghost*, by Adam Hochschild. This book's subtitle, *A Story of Greed, Terror, and Heroism in Colonial Africa*, speaks to the extreme suffering that King Leopold II of Belgium inflicted on the Congolese people. In the mid-1800s, most European countries were competing for land in Africa. Once it was claimed, it was controlled as a colony. In contrast to the practice of all other countries, Leopold privately owned the vast Congo Region. In February of 1885, he announced to the world that he was bringing "civilization" to the people of Congo. Instead, he was brutalizing them to make his own fortune, mostly with ivory and rubber. As Hochschild writes,

Leopold devised a system of terror in which entire Congolese villages were forced to harvest rubber or face death by their Belgian overseers. The women were taken hostage, and many of them starved to death while the men were sent to gather a monthly quota of rubber —and often worked themselves to death in the process.

As I continued my research, in everything I read about this time in DRC history the descriptive words *brutal, barbaric, atrocities,* and *exploitation* were common. During the twenty-three years (1885-1908) of Leopold's rule, millions of Congolese lives were lost to murder, violence, starvation, and rampant disease. His barbaric rule finally became an international scandal, giving the country of Belgium just cause to take over the region's administration. Still, the DRC remained a colony of Belgium until being granted independence in 1960. As recently as 2006, a member of the British House of Commons introduced a motion for the recognition of the Congo Free State's atrocities as a "colonial genocide," calling for the Belgian government to issue a formal apology to the DRC.

Throughout our daily travel, it is easy to see that the country still struggles to survive daily. Even in the capital city of Kinshasa there is only one thoroughfare through the center that has a paved highway. Along that highway are expensive restaurants, high-rise buildings, and billboards displaying beautiful women in gorgeous gowns and perfect make-up. As a visitor, you would think you are in any big city in most any country. Turning right or left, within a block from this downtown thoroughfare, you are immediately reminded of the severe poverty and lack of infrastructure. You once again find huge craters in unfinished roads, street vendors crammed almost on top of one another, with so many pedestrians crossing back and forth it is hard for drivers to maintain any kind of movement toward their destinations. Many of the buildings remain fragmentary and uncared for. There are two completely different worlds, just yards apart.

CHAPTER 4

# Encircled...Overcoming Fear with Joy

*"I have told you this so that my joy may be in you and that your joy may be complete."*

JOHN 15:11

AS I ENTERED my college years, I continued to seek out my life's purpose but still felt unsure of what that truly was. I joined a small group Bible study that met in a college dorm room. This group was part of an international program, Campus Crusade for Christ, committed to teaching and equipping young people with skills for evangelism and discipleship. Through this community, I made friends, all with a common bond of following Christ; many of us were still searching for direction. Within our larger campus community was a group of guys that opted out of dorm life and shared a big old farmhouse. This place became known as "The Farm." We spent many hours playing games in the field and fellowshipping through praise, worship, and prayer time. We gathered around the living room with guitars, an old washboard and even a set of spoons to play music and sing together.

One evening, we were outdoors playing games and sitting around in conversation. As night came upon us, we gathered around in the living room. A couple guys started playing guitars and we all joined in and began to sing familiar praise songs. We continued singing late into the night first with the praise songs, and then, as tiredness set in, silliness followed. The praise songs we started out singing morphed into a series of childhood rhyme songs. We ended with everyone standing in a circle acting out the motions to "Gray squirrel, gray squirrel, swish your bushy tail"!

It was during these years my faith began to take precedence and the choices I was making reflected this newfound assurance.

The sense that I would somehow end up in Africa was not yet stitched into my soul, but God was taking my warp threads and intricately adding his weft threads around my heart, creating a passion for the need to serve.

NOW, AT MPASA, STANDING encircled with so much joy, I felt calmness flowing through me, exchanging my fear with joy. Being surrounded by a sea of black faces was a first for me. Growing up in a small town in northwest Pennsylvania with little to no cultural diversity had not given me the opportunity to experience anything like this before. But this day God was providing for me an experience that would lay the groundwork for what was to come in the world of diversity for me.

Their smiles were so big and bright. The adults were eager to meet us and soon I was enjoying hugs from all. It was like we had been old friends. The children crowded around as well but were shy in allowing me to reach out and touch them. There was so much giggling and clamoring among the little ones to be seen and spoken to. I did not know their language, they did not know mine, but it did not seem to matter. Our communication was not that of words but the joy we were sharing at meeting and making new friends.

The children were dressed in quite a mixture of clothing. Many of the T-shirts had American company names or organizations, championship sports teams, or superheroes. Some little girls were wearing nightgowns or Halloween costumes with Disney princesses. I understood now that the clothing I kept seeing piled on the streets for sale came from the large bales of clothing sent from the U.S. or Europe, through charities. While I was thousands of miles from home, it made me smile to see these familiar icons dancing around on these sweet ones, who had no idea what the words were or for what they stood.

Within a few minutes we walked up into a fairly large room. Shuffling was our only option as we were moving like one sizable ball, with no one wanting to give up their place walking along beside one of these loving strangers.

As we stepped from the bright sun-filled outdoors into the room, our eyes had to adjust to the sudden dullness of light. The room had drab gray concrete walls with small squares for window openings, allowing for an extraordinarily small amount of light to peek in. With the lack of electricity, turning on lights was not an option.

While still standing near the doorway, we had to move quickly to the side, allowing two of the women to haul in the first of two huge cooking pots that stood a little over three feet tall. They were filled with porridge that would warm and fill hundreds of hungry bellies. This porridge (known as *poto poto*) is made with a combination of grains and minerals and cooked over a fire. It is enough for a full day's nutrition as it may be the only meal they receive. It is similar in color and texture to Cream of Wheat.

Bowls were stacked and large ladles were brought in to begin filling them for the waiting children. While this was happening, on the other side of the room, two other women were organizing the children, moving them around like chess pieces, to prepare for singing and prayer before being served. Clapping started as the voices rang out in song. I did not understand the words they were singing but I felt their delight in sharing their song with us. So many voices all together blanketed the room with elation. My earlier apprehensions continued to be washed away, being replaced by the joy expressed by the children. I was eager to know the meaning of the words. Realizing the need for understanding, Adolphe began interpreting for us. It was called *Jesu Azali Awa*.

*Jesus is here.*
*Jesus is here.*
*Jesus is here with us.*
*Alleluia, Alleluia my Jesus.*

At the end of the song Mama Juene closed in prayer as the children prepared to receive their meal.

Marie sat down by one of the big pots as one of the women showed her how much porridge to ladle into each bowl. A spoon was added to each bowl as it was given to each child. Amazingly, they sat patiently awaiting their turn to receive that bowl, but quickly began to spoon it in as they were quite hungry.

Although this was all new to me, it was their daily routine of eating and being nutritionally sustained until the next meal came. Some of the tinier children were held by their moms or older siblings on the wooden benches that were lined along the walls and a few rows toward the back of the room. Young boys and girls with little brothers or sisters carried them around like miniature parents. Several of the girls had them wrapped on their backs in a fabric sling. They were so small themselves, it seemed an impossible task to carry a child on their backs; but they did it with ease. Most everyone sat crowded on the floor as we were carefully tiptoeing and weaving our way through the multitude, handing a bowl to each expectant child.

It seemed to be over quickly. Once they finished eating, bowls and spoons were dropped into one of the empty cooking pots as the children hurried out in the courtyard area to play. I too, wanted to run outside to play, but our team was gathering to begin a tour of the compound.

Dr. Rebecca Yohadi was the director and head doctor of the center. She was a larger-sized woman with an attractive round face and deep brown eyes that sparkled like sun on water. She was wearing a white doctor's coat over her lovely, brightly colored Congolese fabric dress. Her face glowed with happiness to have the opportunity to share the many facets of this ministry. There were several buildings facing a small courtyard with one tree, and with it being the dry season, there were only sprigs of sparse grass causing that gray sandy soil to dust over our shoes as we walked.

One of the things that was necessary for us to know prior to travel was our clothing choices. It was important not to wear something that would be offensive to the culture. Women in Congo are to keep their legs covered and pants are not an option for daily wear. (Nurses may wear scrubs.) Our clothes were long dresses or skirts. Many women there take a piece of fabric and wrap it around with inside and outside tucks and manage to keep in in place without a knot! I was also advised by both my doctor and the team to wear shoes that covered my feet to protect me from parasites in the grass and soil. So, with both a long dress and fully covered feet, I was feeling the heat. A pair of shorts and sandals would have felt good.

The cluster of buildings served as both a medical and nutritional center. As the doctor began to lead us out of the room, she continued to share information about the clinic, with her love for this place beaming through her as she spoke. As we stepped outside the room, we walked a few steps to see a small room piled with bags of grain to make the porridge. Once cleaned, the bowls, cooking pots, and other cooking supplies would also be placed there. Next to that room was the pharmacy for medications used for the patients coming to the clinic. Inside were a few wooden shelves with rows of medicine boxes and bottles, a plastic table, and a few chairs.

Moving closer to the entrance to the compound, we could see a freshwater well, positioned in the center, under a tree. It was not just for the clinic, but for the surrounding community, too. Many people, mostly women, were gathered round waiting their turn to fill their plastic jerrycans and buckets. (The name of the jerrycan refers to its German origins, used around the world since World War II, mostly to carry water.) Again, the scene before me reminded me how resilient these people were. Standing in a line in the burning sun waiting for a turn to fill their jugs and then carry them home; one on their head, and another carried by hand at their side, they still were able to keep smiling and laughing with one another.

The water well was pumped by a foot pedal. Dr. Yohadi asked if anyone wanted to try it. They did it with ease, so I climbed up and started to slowly move my feet like they showed me, but it was much harder than it looked. There was a rhythm along with pressure that was needed to activate the pump. I struggled at first to establish the pattern for my legs and feet to set the needed pace. We all laughed together until I was finally able to figure it out and the water started to flow. Everyone started to clap and shout at my success!

We moved from there to the maternity building, passing small rooms where they had a lab for bloodwork, a surgical room and supply room. I use the terms lab and surgical room lightly as there was no electricity for refrigerated medicines, blood bags, or equipment. The lab was sparsely equipped with a microscope and an assortment of small tools. The room for surgery had a narrow bed and one wooden pole for a medicine bag. I was taken aback by how primitive this all was.

The large maternity room was filled with beds. Young mothers with their babies beside them were lying on almost every bed. The beds were heavy metal with a single brown plastic-covered mattress on top. Some had a sheet draped over, others a piece of fabric. The clinic does not provide linens, as we are accustomed to. Families bring what they have.

Family members sat alongside on the bed or on one of the few plastic chairs scattered here and there throughout the room. Unlike at home, I noticed no young fathers sitting in the room. In the DRC, women are responsible for agricultural production and are completely responsible for all domestic work—including water fetching, firewood gathering, food processing, and meal preparation. Despite the critical role they play in sustaining their communities, women are often treated as subservient and are excluded from community decision-making. The men are the head of the household and spend their day trying to secure a living for their family. They have no time for sitting with the mother and new baby since there are no vacation days or leaves of absence as we are accustomed to having.

Of course, there was no such thing as a cafeteria or vending machines for food. Wrapped together with a piece of Congolese fabric tied with a knot, family members tote meals for the new mom, often sharing the meal together. It usually consists of rice and beans.

Every baby had a full head of beautiful curly black hair lying quietly by the mother's side. There were no cribs. The mammas smiled as we stopped by each bed greeting them and fussing over their precious little ones. Each time I spied one awake, I asked them to hold the tiny bundle and they graciously allowed me a few minutes of cuddle time. As I studied the tiny little faces, I felt rings of tears around my eyes as I wondered what life would bring to this newly cherished child.

Along the back wall at the end of the row of beds, there was one tiny basket-like bed with a thin blanket covering the top. Dr. Yohadi pulled back the small blanket. We peered in, and inside was a tiny set of twins warming in their makeshift incubator. My eyes widened, seeing a kerosene lantern inside to keep them warm.

From the moment I stepped foot off the plane, this trip opened my eyes to what people talk and write about developing countries. Standing here, I felt a moment of disbelief at the tremendous lack of resources they have. Somehow, amazingly, they create ingenious ways to support a better life. Resourcefulness is a way of being. Creativity is born out of necessity.

Across the courtyard was a long narrow building with several open doors. Two rooms were for sick patients or those recovering from surgery. Both men and women were in rooms together. The beds were in rows along the walls as we saw in the maternity room. Family members sat on the cement slab porch outside or nearby on the bed, also like the maternity room. At the far end, the open door was Dr. Yohadi's office. She gathered us into the small front room of her office area furnished with two soft, low-back, navy-blue couches. There was a stack of plastic chairs in the corner.

We shifted ourselves onto the couches. Even with no airflow into the small room with oppressive heat, it felt good to sit down. To our surprise, a tray of ice-cold sodas was brought in along with a tray of freshly shelled peanuts. The ice-cold sodas were a puzzle to me, but we found that a nearby hut had a cooler filled with ice, offering sodas for sale. Where the ice came from remains a mystery.

With Adolphe's help, conversation flowed as we shared with her our team plans for the next week. We brought with us several activities to do with the children, planning to be with them a few more times and assist with feeding the children. Dr. Yohadi was pleased to hear we would be returning and spending more time with them.

As we were soon leaving, I did not have as much time to spend with the children as I had hoped. But we were planning to return tomorrow to spend a longer time and I was bringing a surprise for the children. It quite possibly would bring smiles to the adults too.

We said our goodbyes and headed to our car. Papa slowly made his way toward us from sitting under a cluster of trees at a nearby house. Slowly driving away from the buildings, I looked out the window to see a few of the boys running beside our car waving and smiling. I began smiling and waving out my window. One of the boys reached to take my hand. At that moment, my smile and my heart swelled, knowing a bond with the children had begun.

CHAPTER 5

# Meeting Jubilee...Joy and Realization

*A happy heart makes the face cheerful.*

PROVERBS 15:13A

I N THE LATE fall of my senior year in high school, I started dating a boy who five years later would become my husband. Who knew that while I stood on the stage singing presidential campaign songs during our high school play and he sat below in the pit band playing guitar, that those sparks of "I think I like you" would become a lifetime of knowing "I love you."

As with any relationship, especially because were so young at the beginning, we had our struggles. It is funny, though; I remember meeting Ed for the first time in our seventh-grade year. He happened to be the neighbor and a good friend of my best friend. While I was visiting her house, he came over on his Moped (a motorized scooter). I thought he was cute and already quite self-reliant, as he bought the Moped himself by working two jobs.

Throughout our junior and senior high school years, we ran together in the same circle of friends—never dating each other, but others in that circle. Looking back, it seems as if we were getting everyone else out of our systems before discovering the magical connection we had.

After our graduation, I went off to Behrend Campus, a Penn State campus in Erie, Pennsylvania, about an hour and a half away from home. Ed went to Clarion State College in Clarion, Pennsylvania, a bit closer to home. After his first semester, he discovered that college was not the right fit for him. After my first semester, I figured out that I wanted to teach handicapped children. The college that offered an outstanding program in Special Education was Clarion State College. So, for my second semester, I changed colleges while Ed turned his focus on building a career owning his own store in the growing music industry. He was musically talented and had a personality that drew people in. Going into a business of his own seemed like a perfect fit for him.

For me, the assurance I began to feel through my growing faith was intertwining like a vine with my studies of exceptional children. Each class I took was shaping me into the teacher I aspired to be.

EXCITEMENT WELLED UP INSIDE me as we turned the last bend of the sandy road to the Mpasa Clinic. The giddiness inside me felt like butterflies flitting from flower to flower as I was bringing a surprise with me today. On our final turn into the compound, we could hear the children chanting in their native tongue, "They are coming! They are coming!" We would hear these words many more times throughout the week as we entered. When we came to a stop, children flocked around the car making it hard to open the doors to get out. After just one day, they already felt comfortable with us, triggering my heart to fall in love with them even more.

After our greetings and hugs with the staff, we joined the children inside to sing and prepare for feeding. For any onlooker it would seem like a jumble, but it really was quite organized with everyone knowing what to do. It was just that there were so many people in such a small area. As the children finished, one by one they started to gather outside as I slipped across the courtyard into Dr. Yohadi's back office to prepare for my surprise.

I was a member of a Christian clown troupe called Clowning for Joy. Christian clowning is sharing the Gospel with a whimsical touch, complete with makeup and costumes. Most often the clowns perform in silence, conveying their message through a narrator, signs, and music. Our troupe performed skits during worship, at church functions, nursing homes, and Vacation Bible Schools. Now, here I was thousands of miles away from my troupe transforming into my clown character, Jubilee. I was excited, but anxious at the same time, not wanting to frighten them, as the children, and most of the adults, had never seen a clown before. I decided to bring along my little girl puppet named Felicity, hoping she would help soften their initial introduction to Jubilee.

Jubilee was a burst of colors from head to toe! She had bright yellow hair topped with a hot pink hat with a big yellow daisy on the front. Her pinafore dress was colorful panels of flowers in many vivid colors topped with a sunny yellow T-shirt with appliqué flowers. Peeking out below her dress were matching blue floral bloomers. On her feet, she wore a pair of bright yellow Crocs that matched her hair, decorated with colorful rubber flowers and even a squiggly green worm. Her face had two bright pink circle cheeks, pink lips, long curling eyelashes, and a red rubber flower on the tip of her nose. She put on big smiling face as she exited to meet her new Congolese friends.

The adults from the Mpasa team stood just outside the door, not having an idea of what to expect. After all, they had only known me for one day as Susie, but now I was about to introduce them to someone who looked completely different from the new friend that had entered the room a few minutes earlier. When I opened the door and stepped out as Jubilee, their jaws dropped, their eyes widened, and their faces burst into loud joyous laughter.

Walking slowly and calmly from the adults who had gathered at the door for my initial debut, toward the children waiting on the long cement porch, the wide-eyed stares continued as each child adjusted to this animated, vibrantly colored lady. I gently reached my arm out that held Felicity. She was holding her hand out for them to reach out and shake. One by one they started to relax and soon I could hear giggling. There was one older man sitting among the children on a wooden bench along the porch. His face beamed with pleasure over this curious little puppet and the funny lady that held her. In a childlike fashion, he leaned out reaching his hand out to shake the tiny puppet hand and his smile grew even brighter.

While I continued greeting those waiting on the porch, I entered the room where we had been feeding earlier. The staff was captivated with Jubilee as they were trying to figure out if it really was Susie, their new friend. They each took a turn shaking the puppet's hand, scrutinizing me at the same time. Once I spoke, they knew it really was me. What fun to watch the wide grins appear with this new discovery! Lots of children were seated on the floor with eyes aglow as I stooped down and allowed them to get a closer look at me and shake the puppet's hand. There were a few tiny ones that whimpered with fright, so I moved in directions that kept me from getting too close.

I had a fun little toy to share with them called a Magic Flower. It opened into a pretty paper flower and each time I tapped the stem, the flower changed shape and other colors began to show. Everyone gathered closely around to see that funny little flower. I also brought bottles of bubbles. Each of our team had a bottle, and we all began to blow bubbles into the air. Lots of squeals and laughter filled the room when the children tried to catch them as they blew lightly around the room.

While I continued entertaining everyone, the rest of the team disappeared into Dr. Yohadi's office to blow up balloons for everyone. Once Jubilee finished playing, she joined them. When we walked out into the courtyard with arms filled with the long skinny balloons, it was like an explosion of laughter. Everyone was trying to grab a balloon for fear we would not have enough! Somehow the staff brought some semblance of order to the throng, and we were able to start passing them out. That dusty gray soil was rolling around in great clouds as the balloons and children seemed to be one giant ball spinning around in fits of laughter. The vivid colors of the balloons enhanced the delight that I was witnessing. The simplicity of a balloon can bring such delight.

I stood there still dressed in my costume smiling and sharing the elation of the children. Appearing when I least expected them, blessings came raining down all around.

After having a most splendid afternoon, the dust began to settle as the children started to disperse for home. We packed up our things and headed for the car. The children that were still there, relishing their new playthings, surrounded the car and started moving right along with us. My smile grew knowing that our plan was to give these children a fun-filled new experience, but in truth, I was leaving with a gift too… a heart overflowing with love.

I was no longer just seeing desperation. I saw devotion in a staff spending hours of preparation to be sure every child was receiving daily nourishment. I saw mothers with relief in their eyes to see their children beginning to thrive. I saw hope in every bowl that was served.

CHAPTER 6

# The Congo River...Peaceful

*"I will make rivers flow on barren heights, and springs within the valleys. I will turn the desert into pools of water, and the parched ground into springs."*

ISAIAH 41:18

SINCE OUR ARRIVAL, all our time had been spent in the Kinshasa area, traveling daily from MPH mostly to the Mpasa I Region to be with the children. As I described earlier, Kinshasa is a huge city with constant traffic jams and an overwhelming amount of pollution from the vast number of vehicles. Many of them shoot pure black soot from their exhaust, which swirls around like the smoke from a blazing fire that burns our eyes. With temperatures in the high nineties and our constant travel through the smoggy air, Adolphe proposed we head out of the city and visit the village of Maluku along the Congo River. I felt anticipation building inside me, knowing that we would be introduced to yet another Congolese way of life followed by those who dwell near the water's edge.

Historically, in the DRC, people did not just live anywhere. For their villages, they chose places that were close to the Congo River, either right next to it or within a few kilometers. The river was a source of clean freshwater and many thousands of people relied on fishing. Much of their nutrition came from fish, so the river was also the source of their livelihood, as well as providing some medicinal plants. Their traditional agricultural system was to farm near the river because it provided plenty of water, giving them a natural irrigation system for crops.

This river is an important navigational system in Africa. In the DRC, there are some 8,700 miles of navigable waterway. Of this total, 650 miles are accessible through all seasons to barges.

The portion of the river that runs through the DRC was the setting for *Heart of Darkness*, the 1899 novella by Joseph Conrad set during the brutal days of King Leopold's rule.

In my visit, the farther from the city we traveled, the greener the scenery became, like thousands of emeralds glistening in the sun. With fresh air blowing through the windows, I quickly forgot the smoggy haze of the city. There were big, lush trees hanging over enormous gardens. As we passed the gardens, I saw people dotted throughout the greenery, bending over and working on plots of land overflowing with plants. The rows were perfectly straight, with the people evenly spaced among the large, healthy, rows of plants. It looked like the Garden of Eden.

On the street markets in the city, there are peppers, tomatoes, turnips, potatoes, cassava (manioc plants), and piles of peanuts. Seeing these gardens, I appreciated now where they come from. We had not seen banana or plantain trees, or pineapple plants, but these fruits are native here, as well as papayas and coconuts.

Cassava, in particular, is grown and used in many different ways. The DRC is the world's largest consumer of cassava, which is useful in so many ways it might be called a "magic plant," according to the U.N. Development Programme. It is climate-resistant, growing in both drought and heavy rains. Its roots can be ground into flour for bread and baked goods, while its leaves are a nutritious source of protein and vitamins. The root also finds industrial uses as a source for alcohol and biofuels following fermentation.

While living with Congolese families in my later travels, I experienced the importance of this crop firsthand as we had cassava leaves every day, cooked into a spiced, spinach-like topping served with rice, called *pontu*.

Even though it was more than an hour's drive, the travel seemed easy without traffic jams. The conversation flowed from one topic to the next as we asked Adolphe questions about Congo while he asked about our lives in the USA. He spoke loudly from the front to me in the far back with questions about movies. We found that we were fond of several of the same movies and actors. At the top of our list was Sidney Poitier and *Guess Who's Coming to Dinner*. We laughed as we bantered about the characters and themes.

Continuing our journey, we were amazed by the enormous trucks filled with bags of manioc leaves bound for the city's street-market sellers. The bags were piled high beyond the side rails and often way on the top were goats standing like soldiers on guard, unbothered by the travel. Unknowingly, they too were headed to the market.

Just ahead of us was a sizable mill. As we got closer, we could see large trees were being cut into boards—a sawmill. Adolphe asked the driver to pull off so we could get a better look. Since we were packed into the car, we probably looked like cats trying to make their way from inside a burlap bag as we climbed out of the car. Quickly moving into tourist mode, we pulled out our cameras and began to take pictures. Without notice, like an unexpected summer rain, children came running calling out *mindeli* when they saw the white people with cameras. They wiggled in beside us, hoping to join us for some pictures. Congolese children do not often see themselves, as most have no mirrors in their homes, so camera posing was something new and exciting for them. Making silly faces helped them to pick themselves out as we showed them the view on the back of the camera. Such giggling arose when they found themselves along with the silly faces and poses their friends were also making. Their laughter brought amusement to all over such a simple pleasure. When they saw an adult coming, maybe a parent of one of the children, they scurried off as unexpectedly as they had come.

A short while later, we turned from the highway and started driving slowly down a ruddy dirt road. As the river came into view, we could see the village of Maluku nestled right alongside it. Exiting the car, we walked toward the river through throngs of people who stopped to stare at the strangers who came to their little village.

Standing on the riverbank, I was astonished at the massive width of the river. It was so wide that I could not see the riverbank on the other side, just tall trees in the distance. I was told that the river varied in width from three miles to almost eight miles across.

Sitting in disarray at the river's edge were a couple dozen pirogues, long wooden canoes, each one made from one hand-hewn log. Some were thirty feet long. On the ends inside, the tree's growth rings were visible. Many of them had fishing nets piled inside or draped over the edge, depicting the significant connection of these boats and this river. As we stood there absorbing all that we were seeing, we were elated to find out that Adolphe had negotiated with one of the boat owners to take us for a ride.

Oh! We were going to ride on the Congo River! Since the inside of the bottom of the boat was wet and muddy, the boatsmen brought plastic chairs down and lined them up one in front of the other inside the long boat. One by one we carefully stepped over the side and wove through the chairs to take a seat. It rocked back and forth as we stepped around the chairs. As we paddled away from the shore in this unfamiliar vessel, now seeming quite small, I felt a bit nervous realizing the size and depth of this river… and us with no life jackets.

As we moved along the water, the ride became smoother and swifter. The rocking stopped, so we relaxed a bit, dangling our hands into the water and watching as we created small ripples of water with our fingertips. Marie exclaimed, "I can't believe

I'm riding on the Congo River!" Her exclamation expressed how we all felt.

Floating along, gazing toward the riverbank, my eyes caught bright patches of fabric dotting the shore. Women were working along the bank. Some were bathing their children while others were bending over washing clothes. There were men fishing from boats like the one we were riding in close to the shore. They moved their nets slowly up and down as they tried to lure the fish in. I could hear chatter and laughter travel across the water as they went about their everyday life.

When we returned to the shore, we carefully stepped onto dry land, where small throngs of people were searching the market booths for items to purchase. Women were carrying overflowing baskets on their heads with sleeping children tied on their backs. We were still soaking in the beauty of the culture around us when Adolphe announced he had one more river stop planned for us.

Driving slowly down the road toward our next stop at the river, straight ahead of us, looking like a red clay castle, was a termite mound protruding from the ground about twelve feet. Adolphe explained that this mound was no longer inhabited but that they could stand for years in a petrified-like state. Since we all wanted pictures, knowing we could exit the car without being covered in termites was a relief.

As the river came into view, a collective gasp filled the car. The water had a diamond-like sparkle as the sun began to lower in the sky. There were several thatch-roofed pavilions with picnic tables underneath in a small grassy area near the riverbank. It was the first time since my arrival in Congo that I heard quiet. No cars, horns, or villages filled with people; only the river with the hushed slow paddling of a pirogue boat going by.

In this quiet, surrounded by the beauty of the sun sparkling on the water, I found myself reflecting on all I had been experiencing in this place and the uneasiness I felt upon my arrival. That fear was slowly dissolving into respect, admiration, and a realization that I was falling in love with this country. God had just added another color to my tapestry.

CHAPTER 7

# An Unexpected Connection… A Promise to Keep

*"For where your treasure is, there your heart will be also."*

MATTHEW 6:21

DURING THE WINTER break of my senior year in college, Ed asked me to marry him. Our relationship had grown from high school sweethearts to the kind of love that was meant to be forever. I graduated from Clarion University on May 21, 1977, and the following Saturday we were married at Heckathorn United Methodist Church. Heckathorn was the country church I grew up in, and where my parents continued to worship. Just prior to my graduation, the Special Education Department Chair of the university asked me if I would return as a graduate assistant to supervise some off-campus undergraduate courses. With this offer, my master's work would be paid for by the university. I had not considered going right back to school for my master's, but this opportunity was an excellent one I could not pass on. Two life-changing events in one week.

In our working lives, I was hired as a teacher for the Intermediate Unit in the classroom where I had completed my student teaching. Ed's music store, Harmony Music House, was flourishing. Life as a newly married couple was off and running. As our two lives were now being woven together, the depth of color in my ever-growing tapestry was changing.

AS WE REACHED OUR last day to be with the children and staff at Mpasa, my heart was heavy. I found myself staring out the window remembering that first visit when we wound our way through these dusty trail-like roads. I was anxious then about how I would survive the next ten days. The burden I was feeling now, was wondering how soon I could return.

As we pulled into the Mpasa Center, I needed to push away my gloomy feeling and be thankful for this one more day. Luckily, Jubilee was coming back today to bring another first to the children… face painting. I knew she could turn my clouds into sunshine.

The children were now so comfortable with us that getting out of the car became a bigger challenge. They pressed in tightly, hoping to be the one to grab a hand or piece of clothing before someone else pushed in to take their place. Arriving at this kind of delight was truly cloud-lifting medicine. Once again, we shuffled toward the big room to gather for the meal. The dust billowed behind us as our large troupe moved as one big cluster.

The singing and prayer before the meal was a time of praise for the food and their new friends. As the children clapped and sang Jesu Azali Awa, I felt a rush of knowing Jesus was here with us. We inched through the crowd of children on the floor, handing a bowl to each child. When I looked up from the bowls, I saw a small frail-looking lady standing alone. It was not unusual for mothers to sit on a bench or stand around the outside walls to help feed the tiniest children. But there was something about her that drew me to her.

I walked toward her, and she held onto my arm, looking directly into my eyes. I knew she needed something from me, but I was unable to communicate with her. I motioned to her that I would be back.

With Adolphe's help, I spoke with Dr. Yohadi. She explained that Catherine was extremely sick and needed hospital tests, but there was no money to take her or pay for the tests. After talking with our team, we decided to give them the needed funds for her travel and treatment. Dr. Yohadi was pleased to share the information with her. She smiled as best she could in her weakened condition.

We learned later that she was taken to the hospital the next day, only to discover her heart was failing. Hospital workers drained some fluid that had been building up inside her and gave her some medicine. With our ability to gift them the money, giving Catherine a chance at even a slightly longer life was another life-changing moment for me.

With over two hundred children to feed, the morning flew by quickly. The children gobbled up the warm treat to fill their bellies. While they were finishing, I slipped out to transform into Jubilee, hoping to bring more smiles on our final day.

Gathering outside, the children knew that each day we came something special happened for them. They waited anxiously until Jubilee stepped out to meet them again. This time there was no concern in their eyes, just giggling and grinning. Felicity had so many happy handshakes now; she must have been grinning too!

As the other team members finished inside, we started to line the children up to begin the face painting. So they would understand what we were going to do, we demonstrated by painting on each other. With the sun beating down and the excitement flaring up, faces were dripping with sweat, so we improvised by dusting off and painting arms. The boys loved blue and green snakes wiggling up their arms with a red tongue curling out, while the girls liked flowers, hearts, and butterflies. Taking turns when no one wanted to be left out caused a bit of a hot jam. So, the staff took care of crowd control helping them understand that everyone would have a turn before we finished.

It was quite a feat painting a couple hundred arms, but when we finished even the staff showed off their artwork. Once we cleaned up our paints, we moved to Dr. Yohadi's office to spend some time talking about our time at Mpasa and some other needs at the center with which we could help. We drank cold sodas together, shared stories of our time in Congo with her, and spoke of our hope to return someday.

Reaching behind her, with her radiant smile aglow, Dr. Yohadi dipped her hand inside a hidden bag to pull out exquisitely made matching Congolese dresses for the ladies and a shirt for Wes. The fabric was deep bright gold, covered in bold blue flowers trimmed in green. Large white intricately patterned embroidery flanked the neckline, front, and sleeves, adding beauty to the fabric. Imagine my joy after admiring, almost coveting, the fabrics and dresses I had been cataloging in my mind all my days there. I could not wait to try it on. Luckily, she also wanted to see them on us, so we slipped into the back room and to our amazement each dress fit perfectly! How did the seamstress know our sizes without a single measurement taken?

As we were leaving her office, children were still waiting with the hope that we may have something more to share. Since there were fewer children, we were able to bring out some construction paper and markers to sit and draw with them. I sat on a low wall and placed a paper on my lap with several children gathered around. They each had a puzzled look at the things I had on my lap and in my hands. I gently took the tiny hand of a little girl and laid it softly on the paper on my lap. I held it in place and began to trace around each little finger. Each one standing around pressed in closely to watch as they studied the movement of the marker making colorful marks on the page. When I finished, I lifted her hand and the delight was not just in her face, but also in the others who stood around her. With a smile, I passed out some paper and markers to each to let them see how to make that stick-like thing make marks, but instead they wanted me to trace their hands as well. A few tears pricked my eyes as I realized how unfamiliar these markers and paper were to them.

When this calm and quiet time ended, it was getting late, and we needed to go. We shared tight hugs and a few tears with the staff and promised we would come back. Getting into the car, I wondered how many others might have left with a promise to return. I hoped that my promise would come true.

Our open car windows were filled with the faces and hands of the children who were still with us, wanting one last touch or squeeze before we left. How different they were from our first day together, when the unfamiliar whiteness of our skin brought angst and suspicion. As the car slowly started to move, they followed us out of the center and down the road. As we picked up a little speed, they ran faster to keep up as far as their breaths could take them. My eyes stayed glued to the back window as I watched them grow smaller. A gnawing feeling was rising inside me. I knew I had to keep my promise.

CHAPTER 8

# The Sending Party...A Piece of My Heart

*Search me, O God, and know my heart;
test me and know my anxious thoughts.*

PSALM 129:33

IN LATE FALL of 1983, to my surprise, the Special Education Department at my university called to ask if they could submit my name to Karrin Mancuso, the regional director of Pennsylvania Special Olympics. She was looking for a volunteer area coordinator for four counties in and around the area in which we lived. Already aware of the mission of Special Olympics and the opportunities it offers children and adults with intellectual disabilities was something I wanted to be a part of. It became a huge part of my life for the next eight years.

OUR DAYS WERE SO full of activity on my first visit to the DRC that on our rides home we were too tired to chat. Nourishment and some alone time were a necessity before talking about our day. Once showered, fed, and somewhat rested, we gathered as a team upstairs in the library. It was a time for us to draw together, acknowledging our deepest thoughts, concerns, and discoveries about the culture we were immersed in. It was fascinating to listen to how each of us had had the same experiences that day, yet each of us expressed different emotions and insights.

This evening was going to be different. After dinner, we would be the guests of Bishop Yemba and his wife Henriette, along with local pastors and families at a missionary Sending Party. The bishop felt it was important for those who came to serve the Congolese people to be sent off with a thank you and God's blessings upon them. His staff organized this event in our honor. We were quite excited about the evening. Each day I felt a childlike giddiness that kept swelling up inside me with every adventure.

The bishop's office is the next compound up the hill from MPH, so the ride was quite short. It is a walkable distance, but a bit dangerous in the darkness for pedestrians as the road is narrow and winding, filled with constant speeding traffic. We were guided upstairs to a large room with tables arranged in a U formation, giving it an air of a family gathering. We were seated across the front with everyone facing in for presentation and conversation. Since Karen had been part of the previous team, she had some idea of what to expect, and shared what she knew from her first party. However, she reminded us that the Congolese do not often follow a protocol as Americans do, so this evening might prove to be quite different. Some of us wore the new clothing given to us by the doctor. giving us the look of true Congolese fashion. Entering with us, Adolphe introduced us to pastors and friends

## The Sending Party...A Piece of My Heart

in the crowd, serving as an interpreter as we meandered from group to group.

Bishop Yemba and his wife were already seated at the center of the front table that had been set for us. Adolphe introduced each of us to them individually, allowing us to exchange a few personal words. Soon after, the bishop called for everyone to be seated, so we took our places on either side of him and his wife. I could see along the back wall women quietly scurrying around carrying and organizing pots and pans on a long set of tables covered in Congolese printed fabric. They were making preparations for us to share a meal at the close of the presentation.

Bishop Yemba stood to welcome and greet everyone. He asked each of the pastors around the tables to stand and introduce themselves to us. That took some time as there were many people who came to celebrate with us. Bishop Yemba shared a few words about the importance of the work that the U.S. Partners were doing through ministry with the Congolese. He gave credit to Adolphe as Mission Coordinator and how he was key to keeping the connection between us moving forward to improve the lives of so many in Congo. He then announced that Adolphe would present the American missionary guests, asking each of us to give a short bio and why we had come.

I was at the end of the table, so I was the last to speak. When I stood up, I felt God's presence within me. After briefly giving my name and personal information, I looked at Bishop Yemba and then to the crowd and said that I knew that God had called me to come, but I was unsure when I arrived why I was here. I knew now that the children of the Mpasa nutrition center had stolen my heart and when I left to go home in the morning, a piece of my heart would be staying with them in Congo. As Adolphe repeated my words in Lingala, I could hear soft murmurs of pride among them. I ended with the words, "I don't know when, but I know I will return."

At that, the presentation portion concluded, a blessing over the food was given, and we were invited to the feast. Since we had been eating American food at the guest house, I had not yet seen or eaten any Congolese food dishes. I must say that as I walked down the row of tables filled with all kinds of pots and pans brimming with food, nothing looked familiar. I did not want to offend anyone by taking nothing, so I asked Adolphe to guide me with some choices.

One choice I skipped was the pot of caterpillars. I had seen baskets of these colorful wiggling things on the streets for sale and now seeing them in a pan cooked in a sauce was not exactly high or, better said, not at all on my list to try. I was telling myself NOT to make a face, but to politely say, "no thank you." Adolphe chose a large spoonful for his plate. When we sat down with our plates, Adolphe pulled up a chair at the end of the table near me to tease me with his caterpillar dish. He reached slowly with his fork to poke and pick one up, gradually opening his mouth, and placing it inside with a huge mmmm sound, showing how much he loved the taste. His mischievous display of teasing made me laugh hysterically.

Following the feast, we said our goodbyes to the bishop and his wife and the others we had met throughout our time in Congo. Joy permeated me with such a lovely farewell.

As I lay in bed that night, my mind flipped through pictures of smiles, hugs, and holding little ones in my arms. I thought about our day at the Congo River and the respite it brought to renew and refresh for the days still to come. But mostly I pondered about how I was going to come back. Was this new felt need something God was placing in my heart, or was the excitement of coming to this African country overshadowing God's true reason he brought me here? Eventually, I fell asleep with this question dangling in my mind.

The next morning was Sunday and our final day in Congo. Bishop Yemba chose the church where we were to worship. We found ourselves in one of the most unwelcoming-looking areas of the city. Back a narrow heavily crowded side street, we carefully tiptoed through garbage and trash ankle deep to discover at the turn in the street a little oasis called Bethel United Methodist. Relief spilled over me when I stepped into their sanctuary, a place of refuge and safety. Up until that moment, I felt uncertain about the bishop's choice while walking through the pressing crowd with the smell and mounds of garbage that crunched under our feet. Upon arrival though, we were met with heartfelt greetings and shepherded to the front, where special chairs had been set up for us. Déjà vu from our previous Sunday!

As we immersed ourselves in the music, the language barrier was nonexistent. The music was a mix of native African praise and United Methodist hymns. Using only one drum, singing filled the air. As the ladies' choir sang, their faces were radiant as they raised their voices toward heaven. They captivated me with the beauty of the rhythmic dancing, the striking fabrics, and the voices ringing out as one in harmony.

In the U.S., we tend to set a time limit on worship; we have scheduled times to start and to conclude. The expectation is to be on time and with respect to others, not to keep them too long after the end of the service. We utter a few greetings, and then head out for other Sunday commitments. In Congo, the service times are a suggestion. If the service is scheduled for 10:00, only a few are there at that time: musicians, choir members, and laity. Other congregants trickle in over the next hour. Even the conclusion of the service is not determined by the clock.

The two services we attended lasted for two and three hours. That may seem like a dreadfully long time, but the time flowed like a lazy river that never felt rushed. With numerous choirs, the singing and praise time filled the first hour. Business and announcements, Scripture, and the pastor's message filled the next hour. Then came the offering, which was another period of praise with rhythmic dancing and singing as the congregants went forward to offer their gifts in the labeled baskets on the altar table. This final praise time ended with the benediction.

After the benediction, a most fascinating tradition followed. The pastor and leaders created a line at the door to welcome everyone. But as each was greeted, one by one they joined the line of greeting so that every congregant was greeted by each of the others before leaving. As the last came through, the line was quite long, winding into the cluttered street but filled with smiles and laughter. What a blessed way to leave a service guided by the Holy Spirit and not the clock.

We floated out of the service with spiritual renewal. How perfect to have spent our final day in worship. Since we had not been depleted by traffic and long travel, we spent this time in the car with sharing and discussions. Adolphe was in a talkative mood, gleaning as much conversational English he could from us. He was passionate about speaking English fluently, so he was filled with questions about proper grammar and linguistics. For the first time, I sensed my English Language Arts degree as a blessing.

We returned to MPH with mixed feelings—sadness about leaving, mixed with excitement about the opportunities waiting for us at home to share our experiences with this incredible country and its people. I contemplated all these things as I packed my bags before lying down for my final night of falling asleep to the sounds of Kinshasa.

CHAPTER 9

# Time to Go... Melancholy Blues

*Now may the Lord of peace himself give you peace at all times and in every way.*

2 THESSALONIANS 3:16A

AT THE AIRPORT the next morning, we managed our way through the international travel process and were finally seated awaiting the announcement of our flight. A melancholy lingered around me with an added layer of sadness that made it hard to breathe. It was like a heavy weight had been laid on my chest.

Adolphe was trying to be upbeat, but I could see he also was feeling blue, as his time for the past ten days had been filled with Americans needing him every moment to teach, listen, and learn. Now he, like Cinderella, would be leaving the ball and the conversations that improved his knowledge of the language he yearned to know better. So, the chatter was minimal while the blues were substantial. When they announced our flight was boarding, we said our goodbyes with doe-eyed sadness and tight hugs— hugs that were meant to last until we met again.

My heart was heavy having to say goodbye to this place I now loved, and to my new friend. As Mission Coordinator for the Central Congo Episcopal area, Adolphe worked extremely hard to provide us with the most extraordinary experience, answering our questions and helping us to understand more about his country. Like a shepherd, his primary responsibility was the safety and welfare of this flock of American missionaries, guiding us through our days of tight schedules, while interpreting for us nonstop. My mouth started to curl into a smile recalling his gleaming smile that pulled us through numerous tense moments.

Within minutes we were boarding the bus to take us to the plane. It was the same as when we arrived; hot, crammed, and smelly, but somehow, this time, my senses did not sicken me. In just ten days, my life changed in ways that I never imagined. The things I feared had become things I loved. As I swayed on the bus, I remembered that first bus ride, peering out the window and seeing the soldiers with their guns strapped over their shoulders, walking about with a lofty, proud gait. I noticed them now, but fear had been changed to understanding and with that came compassion.

Again, those haunting eyes from the magazines and then from real-life Mpasa grasped hold of me as I walked across the blistering blacktop to the plane. Not wanting to leave them behind, the heaviness I felt earlier in my chest now encompassed my legs and feet. Mustering up the energy, I lifted one foot up on the first step to the plane followed by another deliberately drawn footstep rising to reach the next step. In vain I tried to lighten my steps until I reached my seat.

I sat now on the plane, leaning back on the headrest, allowing my thoughts to wander. I drift through the past ten days reminding myself how each day unfolded. This mind journey takes me back through that crowded city of Kinshasa. Each time we drove through I tried seeing the people through different lenses. I studied the huge crowds in constant movement, their clothing, the smells, and noted the multitude of sounds. I observed class differences, gender differences, and how those with handicaps were exploited for money.

Now my mind meandered onto the road to Mpasa where I spotted the adorable faces of the children. I remembered them shifting from hesitant to joyful, quiet hidden giggling to rolling in laughter, and chasing us to keep waving goodbye. My love for them surpassed anything I could have envisioned. Regrettably now, I could only hold them in my heart. And this is what I would do until I returned; rejoicing when we would meet again. During these past ten days, I experienced an awakening of who I was or maybe, who I was meant to be.

As the Master weaver continued adding to my tapestry, I could see new depth and colors depicting this new phase. What colors would He add next?

CHAPTER 10

# From the Mountains…
# To the Equator

*Do not conform any longer to the pattern of the world,
but be transformed by the renewing of the mind.
Then you will be able to test and approve what God's
will is—His good, pleasing and perfect will.*

ROMANS 12:2

WE WERE MARRIED almost eight years when our daughter Jaclyn was born May 15, 1985. I had no idea (even though others had shared their parenting joy) that my heart could be so full with love. Becoming a mother meant family, happiness, love, and contentment all wrapped in a tiny bundle. Life for us as a couple quickly changed, but not in a bad way; joy filled our hearts for each other and what this new world was bringing. So we weren't surprised when that same joy filled us up even more with the birth of our son Jim in July 1987.

In the spring of 1989, our pastor called to ask if we would consider being the youth leaders at our church. At first, we thought we would turn it down—youth-aged kids were not my favorite! But God had a different plan. Somehow, with hesitation, we decided to accept; with that acceptance we promised a one-year commitment as youth leaders. That one-year promise turned into seventeen years of loving and nurturing over one hundred young people. A few years later (when we were solidly in love with being youth leaders), we received an unexpected invitation from my friend Mary, with whom I had worked in Special Olympics. Our youth group was asked to join with her church youth group on a weeklong mission trip into the Appalachian Mountains. Her youth had been serving through the Appalachian Service Project, providing home repair and replacement for three summers. I quickly said yes to adding our group to her teams, knowing from her stories what an impact it had on not only the youth, but the adult leaders as well. Now I had to pitch the idea to Ed and some of our youth to make the commitment.

My sales pitch was successful. Our first year, Ed and I took three of our youth, joining the other church youth to form a team. It was a perfect way for us to dip our toes into completely unfamiliar territory and see where God was taking us.

Midweek, we were lying side by side on my air mattress, waiting for our evening gathering, talking about our days so far. Ed looked over at me and said, "It is only Wednesday." I said, "I know." He spoke again and said, "I am never doing this again." I said, "Me neither." But somehow, once again, God tapped His finger on our hearts and by Friday evening, we were talking about next summer's trip! That talking about the next summer's trip continued for sixteen more years. Several of those years, Jaclyn and Jim joined us, making it a family service ministry for us. As they got older, they became crew leaders. From the time they were able to hold a tool, Ed patiently taught them how to use them. From wherever I was in the house, when I would call out to ask what they were doing, the answer always came back, "Helping Dad." Over the years, they both became skilled carpenters. Those were very special years.

Each year upon our return from our ASP trip, Dianne (my former Senior High Sunday School teacher) would ask me how our trip was, and each year, I would say, "It was the best ever!" She would say, "Susie, you say that every year." I would tell her that God would provide something each trip that would flood my heart to the brim with love for ASP and that each year was the best ever. Now I know that when He asked me to dip my toes into unfamiliar water that first year, He knew I would feel that same flood of joy thanking Him for the opportunity.

The funny thing about the ASP trips is that, if I took and separated all the elements that made up the week, they were not things I would normally enjoy. I was not fond of sleeping on an air mattress that allowed cold to creep up through the bottom. Eating school cafeteria-like food and having to pack our lunches each day to carry to our worksite was also not ideal. Cold showers, usually partitioned off with black plastic for some privacy, having no air conditioning in our travel vans after working all day in the sun, and the fact that I really hated to sweat did not add up to the joy I felt. But God knew that joy would override it all. I know now that the years I spent in these lush green mountains were preparation for what God would soon be weaving into my tapestry.

Try and picture yourself standing in the middle of a painted square on the floor like a box. This box is a place where you feel most comfortable in your service to God, like a warm soft blanket or a hot steaming drink makes you feel. This box is filled with service that you feel God has called you to do. You work hard at these things. For example, you love to cook, so taking meals to shut-ins or families in crisis in your church fits nicely inside your box. You realize that taking the meals to those in need is also something you enjoy, so you volunteer for Meals on Wheels. It is a wonderful organization, they need many volunteers, so that also fits inside your box.

This box keeps you wrapped perfectly in the areas of service that you feel called and comfortable to do—areas that are most certainly part of what Christ has called you to do. We like things neat, tidy, and predictable. But God does not always keep things neat, tidy, and predictable in a box wrapped with a pretty ribbon.

What if God is nudging you to step out of that comfortable box? What if He calls you to do something you feel ill-prepared to do? He wants to push and prod us beyond our perceived capabilities. Because our God sees the potential he has placed in each of us, His love will settle for nothing less. The scriptures are filled with Biblical characters that God called to step or even jump out of their boxes and follow Him into uncomfortable unknown territory. Even when He promised "I will never leave you or forsake you," most argued, or even shuddered, at His request, but God reminded them again of that promise. When Moses debated, God had an answer for each of his objections that noted his professed inabilities to do the job. All of Moses' "but, but, buts" were counteracted, followed by God's reminder of His promise to him.

When Moses dies at the end of the book of Deuteronomy, the final two verses conclude with these words:

> Since then, no prophet has risen in Israel like Moses, whom the Lord knew face to face, who did all those signs and wonders the Lord sent him to do in Egypt—to Pharaoh and to all his officials and to his whole land. For no one has ever shown the mighty power or performed the awesome deeds that Moses did in the sight of all Israel.

Moses was only able to step out of his box, follow his call, and complete the journey God called him to do because of that promise. Today, God's promise remains as steadfast as it did with Moses. So, when God was ready to move me from the lush green mountains of Appalachia (which were once outside my box) to the African equator, I had to step out even further, but I was not alone, I was standing on His promise.

CHAPTER 11

# Return... Expand

*The King will reply, "Truly I tell you, whatever you did for one of the least of these brothers and sisters of mine, you did for me."*

MATTHEW 25:40

UPON MY RETURN home in September of 2010, I carried the children of Mpasa in my heart every day. Like a small sea creature clinging tenaciously to another, my soul was cemented to that place. I knew I had to return.

Shortly after I arrived home, I met with my pastor, Jonathan Baker, and shared with him my desire to go back to Mpasa. But this trip would be dedicated to ministering to the children and staff at the nutrition center. With his heart also deeply tied to

Congo, he was delighted to learn that I was eager to return. Missionaries devoted specifically to sharing Bible lessons, making crafts, singing together, and playing lots of games would be something the children had never experienced before.

What I needed most was someone to join me on this adventure. Jonathan and I began to pray that God would allow my vision to become a reality by bringing someone to join me. I began sharing my ideas with friends. Remarkably, my friend John knew someone, through another ministry he was engaged in, that had shared with him she felt called to go to Africa.

With her contact information in hand, I made a call to her. Once we connected by phone and I shared my first African experience with her and the vision I had for a second trip, she was eager to join me. Both our prayers were being answered. Beverly Bynes would be joining me.

Over the next several months, Bev and I talked and met many times. Each time, our excitement grew as we began to plan all the things we wanted to share and do with the children. Jubilee would return bringing bubbles for every child. My friend Bill had hundreds of bright yellow duck-shaped bottles of bubbles on a string necklace he had earmarked for our children. Beverly, a singer and guitarist, began preparing simple praise songs we could share in English, as they loved learning new English words.

Entering the Democratic Republic of the Congo requires a visa, a letter of invitation, and mounds of paperwork to carry with you while traveling in the country. Beverly and I spent time preparing all the needed documents and then eagerly awaiting the return of our passports with the coveted visa stamp. Finally, with all our papers in order, July 22, 2011 arrived, and we were on our way to the DRC. It is about a 24-hour travel schedule so our arrival would be the next day.

I prepared Beverly as best I could for the early darkness, oppressive heat, soldiers and police with machine guns, and the overpowering smell of exhaust mixed in with burning garbage in the city. But even with my precautions, it dazed her. Once we were through the long, congested customs line, awaiting us on the other side was that peace-giving smile of Adolphe Yamba Yamba.

Relief washed over me to see it shining through that crowd once again, just as it had on my first visit.

As we journeyed through the city, my mind flooded with an avalanche of memories that brought a smile to my face and gladness to my heart. We arrived at MPH to see the welcoming faces of Clay and Cindy Dunn with a lovely meal awaiting us. Clay had been remodeling guest rooms and we were in one of the newest makeovers with its own bathroom. There would be no more walking down the hall to share one large bathroom. As we began to settle in, I quickly fell asleep to the sounds of Kinshasa that had kept me awake on my first visit.

Adolphe met us the next morning (Sunday) announcing we would be walking to the bishop's office building just up the road for our church service. He asked Beverly to bring her guitar as many in this church were English speakers. The service was upstairs in a large room decorated with brightly colored drapes that hung from ceiling to floor across the front of the room, with rows of chairs filling the rest of the space. As we entered, it was filled with people, but we were ushered to the front where seats were prepared for us.

I was captivated during the opening hour of music and song, soaking in its beauty as I had the year before. This service was one that was done partially in English. The choirs danced and sang. The Kamana Family, a group of five siblings, sang a cappella. Their harmony was so perfect it was as if they shared one pair of lungs. The youngest boy had the voice of an angel. When he sang, it was like floating on a cloud.

Beverly was asked to share some songs with her guitar. She sang out in praise as the congregation joined in with her. For someone experiencing Congolese worship for the first time, Bev seemed as if she had always been a part of it. She had an instant connection with the Kamana Family. During our time there, she spent several evenings singing and playing guitar with them, each sharing songs with one another.

Monday morning, feeling like a child on the first day of school, my anticipation grew with each turn in the road. Our driver worked the steering wheel like a pro-racing driver, twisting us through the deeply rutted sand. We were on our way to the Mpasa

Medical and Nutritional Center, the place where my heart lay nestled in warmth from last summer.

As we continued to wind our way through the sandy trail-like roads, I was drinking in the familiar sights and smells around me, easily recapturing that feeling of contentment I had carried back home.

Once we reached the nutrition center, children were everywhere. Scattered among them were some of the familiar glowing faces of the women who serve them each day. As I opened the door, children crowded around, reaching out a hand hoping for me to at least touch it. But for me, just touching a hand was not enough. I needed to caress each face and share smiles and giggles with each one. I embraced each woman in a tight rocking hug with laughter and kisses mixed in as we looked closely into each other's eyes, knowing the friendships we began last summer were instantly renewed. Dr. Yohadi stood with that radiant smile awaiting her hug. This was an incredibly special hug. One that I thought about many times over the last year, hoping to rekindle our friendship. Beverly was quickly scooped into the crowd feeling the pull of electricity generated by our bliss.

Together, we made our way slowly with the crush of children in tow, and entered the large room where the daily bowls of food were served. Children were crowding in, some sitting on the floor and some on the few wooden benches. It seemed like lots of confusion, but the women went about their work as if there was perfect order. I stood in the middle of this organized confusion picking up children, holding each for a few minutes and then lifting another while many of the older children stood closely around me. Most were giggling at hearing me speaking English once again; some were touching my hair with a chuckle, as it felt so different from their own.

While bending down to place a little one back on the floor, another stood there with his hands held up to me. He seemed so small amongst the jumble of children clamoring around the room. He studied my face so carefully—probably because of my whiteness. When I lifted him up, just as I had so many others already, he clung very closely to me. It felt different somehow.

It reminded me of a line from the movie *Sleepless in Seattle*—"and when we touched, it was like magic." While I was still holding him, Dr. Yohadi came over with a broad grin on her face. Maybe she already saw the connection we felt. She told me his name was Miriam and she was two years old. He was a she! With her head shaved close, and wearing boy's clothing, I had assumed her to be a boy. Dr. Yohadi just smiled at her in my arms.

I placed Miriam on the floor near her older brother Shako to eat. He was the one who brought her each day for them both to receive their daily bowl of nourishment. I then joined the staff to serve, as the children were eager for their food.

After we finished, Beverly was prepared to share a Bible story with large poster illustrations for the children to view while listening. Even though the room was filled, it was as quiet as a library as they waited for the story to begin. Bev would read a few sentences while Adolphe interpreted. The afternoon went by so quickly as the children were engrossed in the story telling and the pictures. Even the staff stood mesmerized at the back. With Beverly telling the story and Adolphe interpreting, it was a whole new experience for everyone.

Miriam continued to be in my arms most of the afternoon. She did not want me to put her down. She kept her legs wrapped around my waist and her arms around my neck. When it came time for us to prepare to head back to MPH, she reluctantly let go of my neck as Dr. Yohadi took her from my arms.

In comparison to 2010, traveling back and forth was much longer. Construction had begun downtown on the route we took each day, jamming the traffic into fewer lanes than usual. It was still hot, muggy, and growing dark, but we did not mind as we spent the time recalling the events of the day with relaxed contentment. The day had been filled with delight for us and the children.

Each day we traveled there to help with the mealtime, and then spent the rest of the afternoon doing special things with the children. Some days we played games, sang, read a story, or made a craft, like wands with ribbons and bells for dancing. Jumping rope was a popular event as the children made a competition out of the number of jumps before missing. But when Jubilee made her appearance, the level of joy increased as she passed out the bright yellow duck necklaces filled with bubbles for everyone. Bubbles always bring spontaneous laughter as they float like little glowing rainbows reflecting the light; most especially when many are experiencing them for the first time.

As we drove into the compound each day, the children were waiting, but there was one little one who was watching specifically for me. On day three, Miriam watched from a distance as our car pulled in. She began waddling toward me, crying loudly. When she stopped at my feet, I picked her up. She immediately stopped crying and laid her head on my shoulder with both arms wrapped tightly around my neck and legs cinched around my waist. A deep connection was forming between us like a lock and key. Even the staff detected something more as she waited each morning for me to come and cried each day as they took her from my arms when I left. They began to call her the "little monkey" as she embraced me like a baby monkey clutches onto its mother. It seemed an unforeseen connection for her to attach herself to someone so quickly whose appearance was unfamiliar and so unlike her own.

For our second Sunday morning worship, we went to the little Mpasa church held in the big room where we fed the children. The congregation sat on the wooden benches while we were shown to the plastic chairs set up along the side near the pulpit. The placement of the chairs allowed us to easily see the congregation and those still coming to join us. Once the service started, I was looking toward the front while the pastor introduced us as we stood and shared a few words about our experiences during our time spent in Congo. Dr. Yohadi presented Beverly and me with beautiful United Methodist scarves. Once seated again, I heard a little one start to cry, and when I looked back, there stood Miriam with Shako stooped behind her, trying to keep her from coming up to me. I motioned for him to let her come. She toddled up, with tears falling, until I picked her up. Her tears stopped and the congregation murmured with a bit of amusement when they saw her so contentedly wrapped in my arms.

That day I learned that Miriam lived with her father and Shako, her older brother by twelve years. Just the three of them lived in a tiny green tar paper house on the road close to the nutrition center. Miriam's mother had left when she was seven months old, and Shako's mother had been gone since he was much younger. Because their father was a soldier and worked every day, Shako was responsible for caring for Miriam; therefore, he was unable to continue going to school. He told me that his father asked him to choose between continuing his studies or caring for his sister. He chose to care for his sister. He took her with him wherever he needed to go. His friends called her his "backpack" as she was always on his back. His story opened my eyes even more to the harshness of their lives and having to make grown-up decisions while still just a child. Unanswerable questions began to bubble up. How was I ever going to leave her when it was time to return home? What would it be like for her each day that I did not return?

As we began our second week, we followed the same pattern as our first, spending each day with the children. The difference was the familiarity we now had with one another. Even the people of Mpasa who lived near the road we traveled each day were used to seeing the two white ladies going by. Soon, they were waving and smiling knowing we were bringing so much happiness to their children. When our car was in sight, the children began calling out our names with some of them running alongside the car, with others trailing behind as we made our way through the gray sand-filled roads.

One morning, the girls decided to teach us one of their games. The staff joined in too to help steer us through the motions. It was a hilarious time as we tried to follow the game rules of stealing someone from one team to the other, chanting and turning our backs to the opposite team trying to keep the captured one from being caught and taken back.

With no word in the Lingala language for goose, our version of duck, duck, goose, became the game of chicken, chicken, duck, or in Lingala, *pso pso, pso pso, libata*. I certainly got my exercise in as everyone was relentless in wanting me to chase them. Laughter could often be heard all around as the game became a favorite to play.

Jumping rope was also popular. We made huge circles with the person jumping the rope in the middle as we all counted in unison the number of jumps before missing. Everyone wanted a turn. We soon found out that we needed to create several circles of competitions with so many children and levels of abilities. The boys were the most competitive and barely able to contain themselves, waiting for another turn to beat their last jumping score or the latest winning number. Miriam's brother Shako was the fastest and almost always had the highest number of jumps. For the first time, as I stood in the circle watching, I saw them as just children. Up until this moment, I kept seeing them as poor children in need, but now, like the scales removed from Saul's eyes, I was seeing them as children. God had opened my heart when I arrived, and now, He was opening my eyes.

Each morning when we entered the compound, Miriam was waiting for me to pick her up and carry her with me all day. When she fell asleep on my shoulder, as she did every day, we would lay her down, but as soon as she awakened, back she came into my arms. I was sure when I was dressed as Jubilee, she would be afraid or not know who I was, but right up she came and stayed until she slept on my shoulder once again. Every afternoon when I left, she had to be taken from my arms. Something deeper was happening between us, but I was unsure what to think of it. At this point, I had no idea the plan God had for me. What was He weaving into my tapestry?

Throughout our days there, we took many pictures of the children, so on our last day, we decided to surprise them with a slide show. I had brought a projector from the U.S. for Adolphe to have for his classroom at the university where he taught nursing classes. We had a gas-powered generator at Mpasa that we could use to power the projector. I purchased a big piece of white fabric to hang on the wall for our screen.

Most of the children had no mirrors in their homes, so seeing themselves on the small screens on our digital cameras had been something new for them. After a while, they began to do something different each time a camera pointed in their direction, trying to create a pose so they could easily stand out. Once we gathered them inside and projected the first picture on the wall, one massive roar of laughter rang out at seeing themselves so large on the screen. With each slide showing a different face, the roars continued. The absolute joy in that room was contagious. The staff too, anxiously waited to see themselves pictured bigger than life. As I gazed from the screen to each face aglow around the room, my smile grew so bright, I felt like I too, was glowing like a neon sign.

Before coming on this trip, my friend Susie gave me a cross necklace to wear as a reminder of her daily prayers for me. I wore it every day to keep her prayers close to my heart. As I was preparing to leave Mpasa for the last time, I decided to place the necklace around Miriam's neck as a reminder to Miriam's family that I would be in prayer for them. Shako understood my affection and smiled, knowing the love I already had for them both. I was trying hard to hold back tears as we said our goodbyes to the staff and children. This was much more difficult than my goodbyes from last summer as the bonds had grown exponentially during these two weeks. Our hugs were longer and tighter, our eyes were filled with tears, and our hearts were heavy.

Driving away, tears continued to fill my eyes as the children ran along beside us, grabbing our hands and calling our names repeatedly. The same question arose again in my mind...when would I be able to return?

Our final evening ended, much like that with our 2010 team, with a large "Sending Party" hosted at the bishop's compound. Adolphe introduced us, then Bishop Yemba spoke about the beauty of having missionaries come to be with them in partnership to improve the well-being of the children and their families at Mpasa. When it was my turn, I reminded them of my departure in 2010, when I knew somehow that I needed to return. When God gave me this opportunity to be back with them, my heart filled with gratitude to be able to be there once again. I continued by telling them that the people of Congo were burned deeply into my heart and that a second piece of my heart would remain with them until I returned.

As Beverly and I settled into our seats for the first leg of our journey home, I laid my head back to rest. As things quieted around me, without warning, melancholy welled up from deep inside while tears dripped softly down my cheeks. I could still feel Miriam's tiny arms wrapped around my neck. I reached up and touched my own hands to my neck envisioning her presence. How had this tiny little creature reached so profoundly into my heart?

CHAPTER 12

# Unexpected...Perfect

*In their hearts humans plan their course,
but the Lord establishes their steps.*

PROVERBS 16:9

"TRUST ME, MY Child," He says. "Trust Me with a fuller abandon than you ever have before. Trust Me, as minute succeeds minute, every day of your life, for as long as you live. And if you become conscious of anything hindering our relationship, do not hurt Me by turning away from Me. Draw all the closer to Me, come, run to Me. Allow Me to hide you, to protect you, even from yourself. Tell Me your deepest cares, your every trouble. Trust Me to keep My hand upon you. I will never leave you. I will shape you, mold you, and perfect you.

Do not fear, O child of My love, do not fear. I love you." - Amy Carmichael, missionary to India

Traveling for a week each summer with our ASP teams brought a new set of challenges, many of which I thought I would not be able to adjust to. I did not like cold showers, sometimes in one large open shower in a high school locker room; cafeteria food that most times was overcooked; packing the same lunches for the day to eat at the worksite, and sleeping on an air mattress in hot school classrooms. I especially hated to sweat. Somehow though, I managed to come home each time ready to go back. The relationships we built with our teams, the families we worked for, and the new friends we made with other groups outweighed those challenges. Even God knew that I really hated to sweat, but He ignored that fact and planted a seed that took me to the equator, where sweating was inevitable.

LEAVING CONGO BEHIND BROKE my heart. I was tied to these people in ways I never thought possible. My mind was constantly floating back across the ocean. Once home, I shared with Ed that I was not sure that I could wait a whole year before going back. He understood me so completely, as he knew the tenderness of my heart. With a little glimmer in his eyes, and a slight smile on his face, I could tell he had something brewing in his mind. He had a proposal. Because I was a teacher with a Christmas break, I could leave right after Christmas, and spend time in Congo as a Christmas gift from him. This inspiration touched deep into my soul. Instead of a twelve-month wait, it would be only six months.

Soon after, I met with Jonathan, and we talked about my return at Christmas time. He wanted to help me make it happen. His big concern for me was I would be alone on this trip. He felt it would be better for me to stay with someone instead of at the MPH Guesthouse. After sharing this with Adolphe, he talked with Dr. Yohadi, and she offered her home to me to live with them. It was a perfect idea as she lived much closer to Mpasa, saving a lot of time traveling, and I would be safe with her family. The guesthouse offered filtered water for drinking, familiar American food, clean hot showers, and towels, but to be sure this stay would be quite different. My ASP experiences were going to be put to the test!

On December 27, the plane took off from Dulles Airport in Washington, D.C., with my heart fluttering with anticipation. Tomorrow I would be landing in the place where pieces of my heart remain. After landing and going through that stern-faced gauntlet of customs agents, I entered the airport baggage claim at the N'djili Airport in Kinshasa. There was Adolphe waiting with that beaming smile, making me feel like I was home.

Traveling to Dr. Yohadi's was a much shorter trip from the airport, just seven kilometers as compared to twenty-six to the guesthouse. She lived on the outskirts of Kinshasa, off the main highway through a maze of narrow roads with many turns and bends crowded with walking people. The road was wet in places, and black mud layered with garbage all along our route made me feel uneasy. On the final turn, our car shimmied down a steep rutted road and there at the end stood Dr. Yohadi, with open arms and the infectious smile and laughter I remembered so clearly. Beside her were her three children, Israel (called Isa), Arnold, and Tina, her mother, and her brother Alphonse and her sister, Dada. Behind them was a high metal gate that, when I walked through, revealed a lovely home ready for a guest. She had prepared her bedroom for me with a large bed covered with mosquito netting, an air conditioning unit (which worked when they had electricity), a bathroom with running water (when it worked) and a flushable toilet with a plastic garbage can next to it filled with water for when the faucet water wasn't running. After the tour, I felt relief and could not have been happier with my accommodation.

After discovering that the mornings never had running water from the faucet, nor working electricity, I quickly learned this was something I had to prepare for ahead of time. So, the night before, I always made sure my buckets were full and reminded myself that I would not have a hair dryer for styling my hair. I had already learned that with no filtered water, I had to use bottled water to brush my teeth. I surprised myself at how easily I was adjusting.

Even though the house had tiled floors, bedrooms, a living room, and a dining area, the kitchen area was outside. The stove was a small charcoal fire. Just a dirt floor, with a couple small wooden stools for sitting on while preparing the meals, made up the cooking area. I was amazed each day that such beautiful meals had been created with bare necessities over a small charcoal fire.

Traveling to Mpasa from here was easy, arriving quickly at the turn-off to begin the trek on those now familiar sandy roads. Shortly after we started winding through, I could see little ones running toward our car and shouting "Susie, Susie!" Oh, how it made my heart soar to hear my name being called out in shouts from little faces beaming up at us with huge spontaneous smiles.

As our car came to a stop, instantly the children crammed up against the car blocking the opening of doors. When I finally was able to open my door, there stood sweet handsome Shako with Miriam in his arms, and my necklace still around her neck. She put her arms out for me to take her. When I lifted her to me, her arms went around my neck while her legs wrapped tightly around my waist. Tears came to my eyes. It was like we had never been apart—lock and key once again. Although there was much chatter and excitement happening around me, for a few moments, there was silence as I gazed into this child's eyes. I was remembering the first time I picked her up and held her in my arms. A soft loving hug from my friend Jeune brought me back to see the crowd of children and adults awaiting my greetings. As in my past visits we made our way together to the big room.

Inside, we began the feeding ritual with singing through grinning faces mixed with giggling, all of us bursting with happiness to be in this place together again.

Adolphe's home was close to Dr. Yohadi's home, so traveling to Mpasa each day for him, too, was simpler than when he had to make the trek first to MPH. This allowed all of us to spend more time each day at the center.

I loved being enveloped in the Congolese culture. Instead of a 6 pm dinner at MPH, with the rest of the evening talking with other guests or being in our rooms, I spent the evenings at a more personal level, visiting with Dr. Yohadi's family and learning more about Adolphe and his family. After a couple of days, I learned that their meals were based around rice and cooked cassava leaves with fish or chicken, almost always including cooked plantains. Occasionally there was some beef. Most families did not have the luxury of meat, but Dr. Yohadi had a regular income with both her sister and brother also living there, contributing to the food budget. As an eating house guest, I insisted on adding to the budget, too. Her sister Dada was an excellent cook and created wonderful omelets in the morning alongside the freshly baked bread found at the markets nearby. Their mama was also part of the household and cooked the evening meals for everyone. There were two meals a day for a family whose income could afford it.

One of my first days at Mpasa, I shared the Christmas story. I brought nativity stickers that paired with a stable setting for each child to create their own nativity scene. It was the first time for them to see and use stickers. Watching their faces light up as I demonstrated how to use them was incredibly fun. It was a delightful afternoon as the children spread out all over the floor with some using the benches as tables. They worked intensely moving the stickers around until they made a perfect scene, each needing to share their final creation. When they left for home, I could see their excitement to show their families what they had made.

The next day, Jubilee came dressed in her new Christmas outfit, sporting a bright red hat that set off her bright red shoes and Christmas-patterned dress and pantaloons. She brought jingle bell necklaces made by my class at school. They strung and hung over two hundred necklaces to share with the children. My students were pleased to be making something to share with children across the ocean. Passing out the necklaces was a grand time with the extra added fun of jingle bells tinkling around everyone's necks. She also brought more balloons and this time she had bubbles from a bubble gun that produced tons of bubbles all at once, causing a frenzy of laughter while chasing and catching them. She passed out bright green heart-shaped stickers that said, "I hugged a clown today." Everyone wanted a hug to get to wear that pretty sticker. Later when I looked around, everyone was sporting a bright green heart.

Miriam stayed by my side throughout each day. Even when Jubilee went to visit the new mothers and babies, she tagged along in her arms. She did not like it when Jubilee held the new babies. Her face showed distaste with the idea that another child was in the arms of the person she had established as her own. We toured the rooms with patients who had surgeries or were sick, and visited with their families. We listened to Dr. Yohadi as she explained the medication room and distribution program. All the while, Miriam stayed content in Jubilee's arms.

When I arrived home from my summer Congo trip, I had created a small photograph album of pictures of Miriam and me together. I brought the book with me, hoping to meet her father and give it to him. Therefore, I was thrilled one afternoon when Adolphe introduced him to me. He was tall, with kind eyes and a gentle-spirited personality. I chatted with him for a while and then presented him with the book and some money for him and his family (a suggestion from Adolphe). Later, while playing with the children, I saw him sitting on a bench looking page by page through the album adding a smile to his face. The pictures told the story of love I shared with Miriam.

The eight days went by too quickly and I found myself at the point of saying goodbye once again. Having so much personal time at Mpasa cemented my relationships with the staff. I knew everyone by name now while sharing about our families with one another. I discovered which of the children that came to eat belonged to them. The days were sweetly filled with building friendships. On the last day, everyone crowded into the doctor's office. I was presented with a gift especially from them. It was a wood carving of a mother holding a baby in her arms, with their heads touching. They told me they chose this gift because I was the "mother of all the children at Mpasa," wanting me to always remember them even when I was home across the ocean. Tears were shed by all as we said our goodbyes already hoping for my return in the summer.

I had one more event before leaving the next morning. Adolphe took me to his home to meet his family and join them for dinner. Not only was his family there, but some good friends as well. Sitting around a long table, I was asked many questions about my life and family, with the conversation switching from English to Lingala and some French as each chose to speak in their preferred language. Adolphe was kept extremely busy interpreting throughout. It was an evening filled with enjoyment and relaxation.

Adolphe told me that it is an important event when a Congolese family entertains a white person. People who observe it see the hosts as important people as well. He said it was true too for Dr. Yohadi when she welcomed me into her home. I learned so much about their culture during this visit.

After saying goodbye, my feet felt like they were strapped with weights as I walked outside the airport toward my waiting plane. I thought back to my first visit, nearly two years ago, wondering when I would return. I had made two more trips since then and each time I felt that heaviness under my feet and in my heart as I dragged myself up the steps. My goodbye to Miriam left a gaping hole in my heart, making me wish I could take her home with me. While the plane was still sitting on the ground, I thought about planning my return. My mind flooded with moments from my days here, each adding a new dimension to my experience. How was my tapestry changing? What would the next threads to be woven look like?

A typical mama with her baby on her back readying to place her basket on her head (Summer 2010)

Susie with the children of Miriam's Table (Fall 2016)

Beverly is sharing her first Bible story on her second day at Mpasa. Miriam is attached to Susie (Summer 2011)

A child coming from the river near Miriam's Table (Summer 2014)

Miriam has taken another little one in her arms (Summer 2019)

Miriam feeding a little brother at Miriam's Table, so his big sister can eat (Summer 2019)

A sunset in the village of Wembo Nyama (Summer 2021)

Susie feeding Miriam for the first time. Obviously, she was not fast enough as Miriam took the spoon from her and started feeding herself (Summer 2011)

A home in Mpasa we passed each day (Summer 2011)

Dr. Yohadi proudly displays the inside of the building of Miriam's Table just prior to opening day (Fall 2014)

The view from the top of the hill above Miriam's Table (Summer 2023)

Adolphe is teasing Susie at the Bishop's party while eating caterpillars (Summer 2010)

A sunset in the village of Diengenga (Summer 2023)

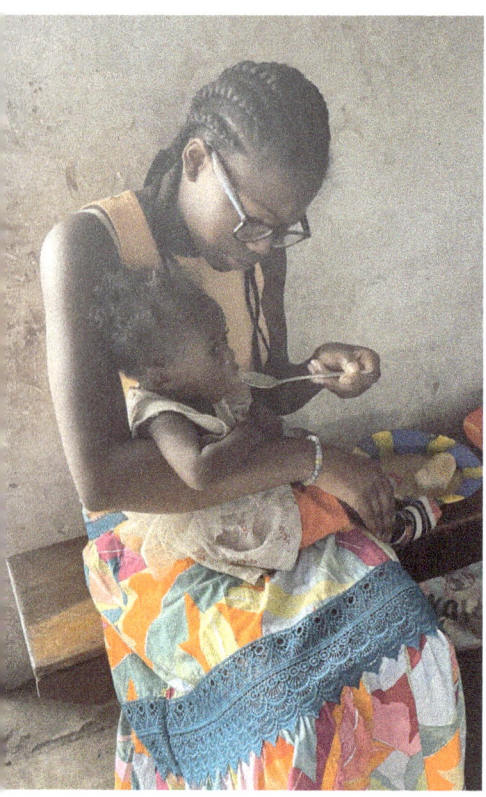

If you are looking for Miriam, you will find her holding or feeding a child (Summer 2023)

A sunset in the village of Okitodimba (Summer 2023)

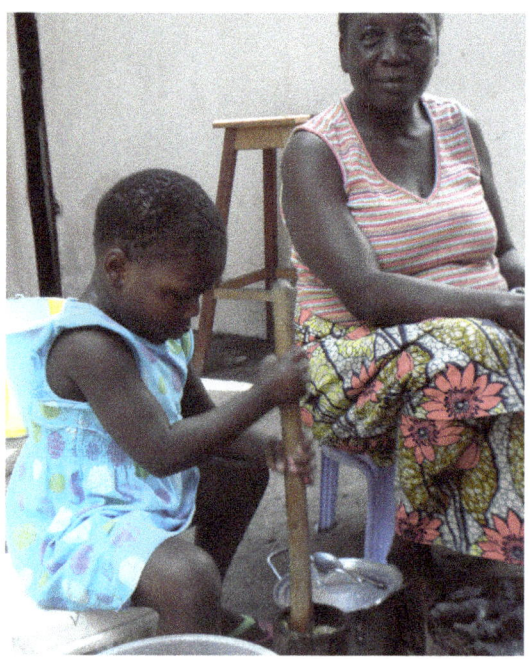

Miriam is helping in the kitchen at Dr. Yohadi's with Koko (Fall 2013)

Miriam as a little mama (Fall 2013)

Miriam is enjoying a picture book while Susie continues to wait for her exit visa (Fall 2013)

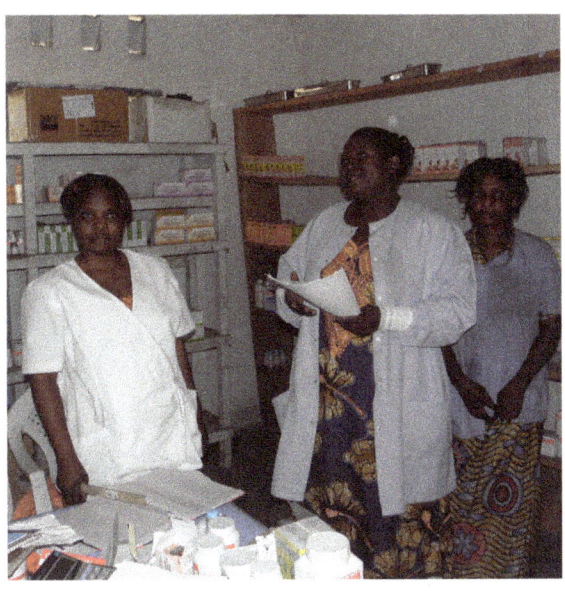
Dr. Yohadi and two staff in the medicine room (Summer 2011)

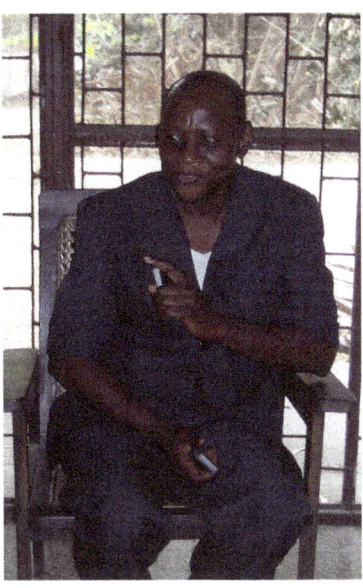
Dr. Adolphe Yamba Yamba, Congo Partnership Mission Coordinatpr (August 2010)

At the Mpasa Nutrition Center, this young girl cares for her three younger brothers and sisters (August 2010)

Adolphe, Beverly and Susie talking and resting after a relaxing walk around a lake outside of Kinshasa (Summer 2011)

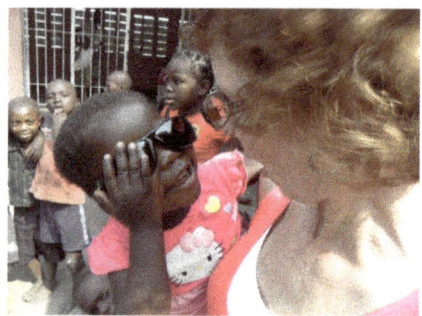

Miriam wearing Jaclyn's sunglasses (Summer 2012)

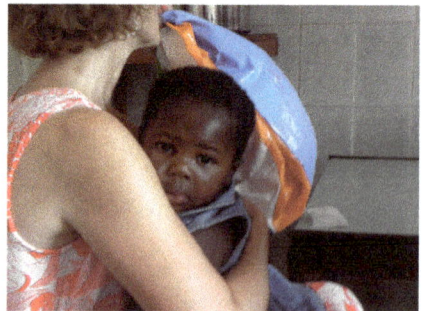

Miriam and Susie (Summer 2012)

Miriam enjoying her poto poto (Summer 2012)

Miriam is playing going to market (Fall 2013)

Miriam's home in Congo that she shared with Shako and her father (Summer 2012)

Susie trying to pump the well at Mpasa, but struggling to get the rhythm right (Summer 2010)

Miriam and Susie on their second day of magic (Summer 2011)

Miriam's first day with her new dad in Congo (Fall 2013)

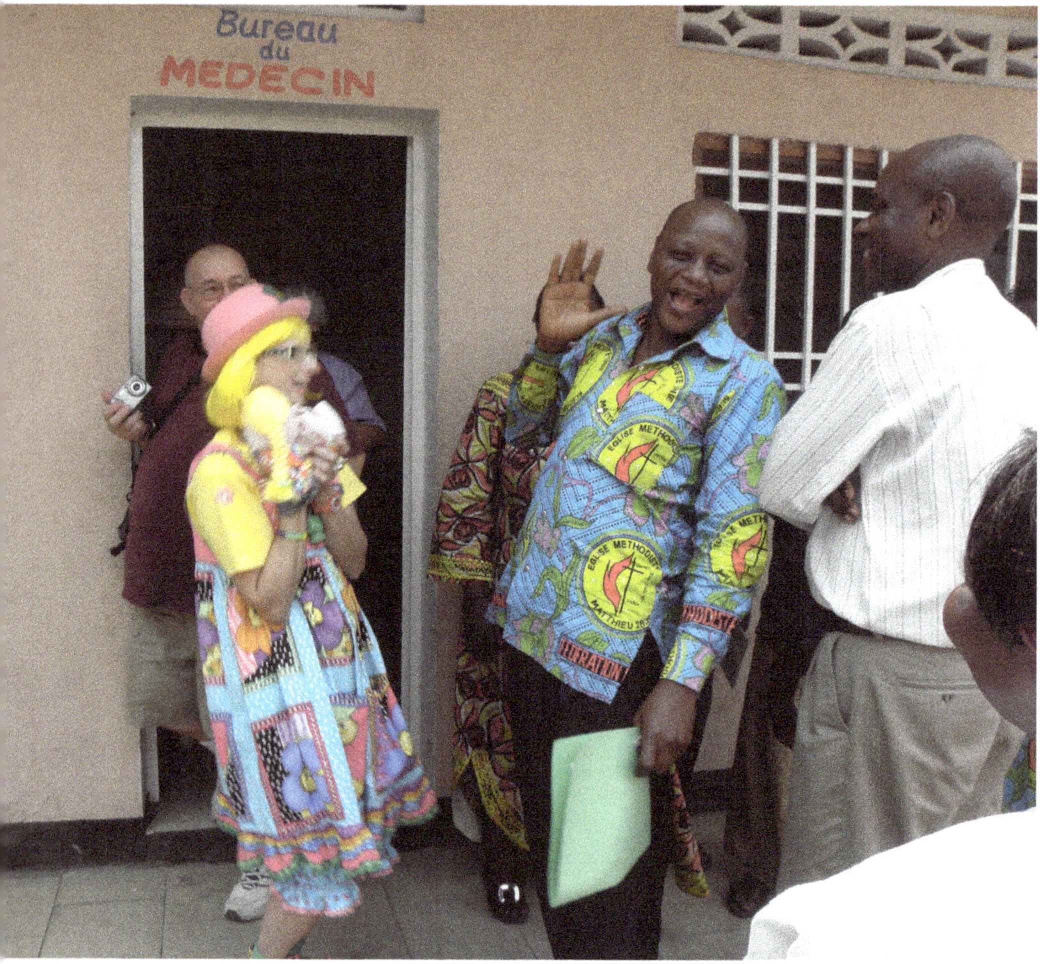

Jubilee received quite a surprised reaction when she stepped out for the first time (Summer 2010)

Miriam is showing everyone she is strong enough to take her suitcase to the airport entrance (Fall 2013)

Miriam enjoying time with her soon to be big sister, Jaclyn (Summer 2012)

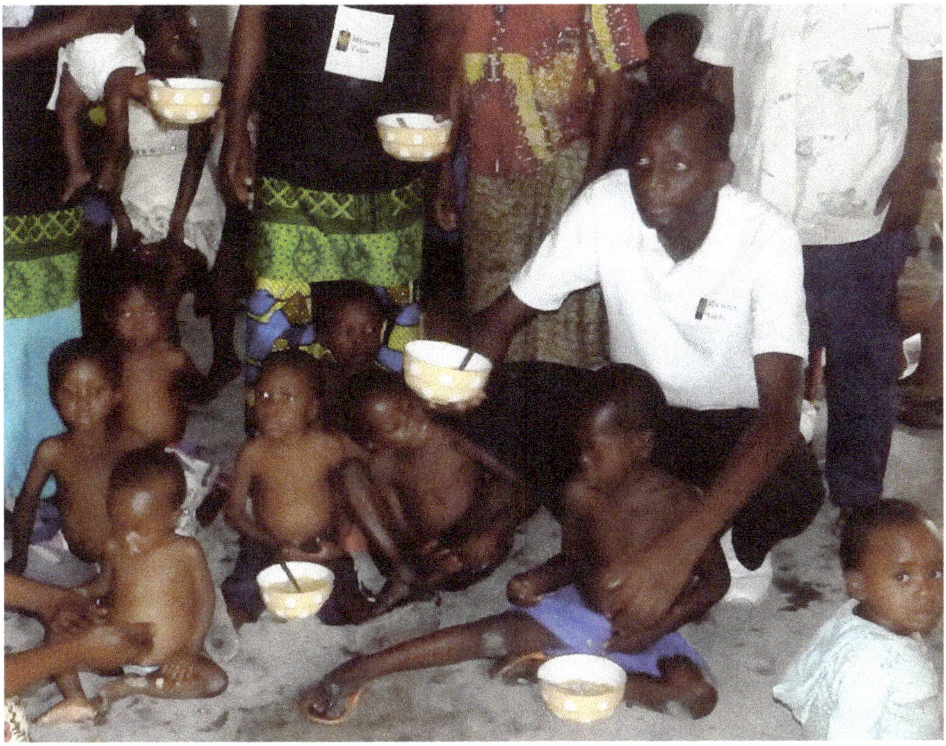

Opening day at Miriam's Table with its director, Alphonse (Fall 2014)

Miriam's Table today (Summer 2023)

Crowded Kinshasa street scene

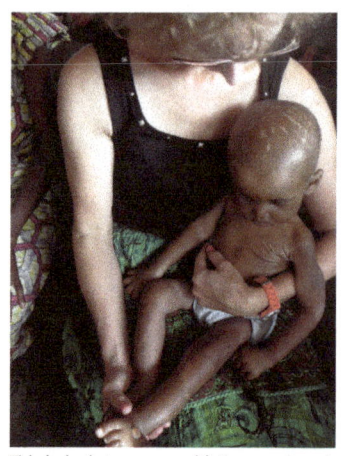
This baby is two years old. He was placed in the severely malnourished program (Sumer 2011)

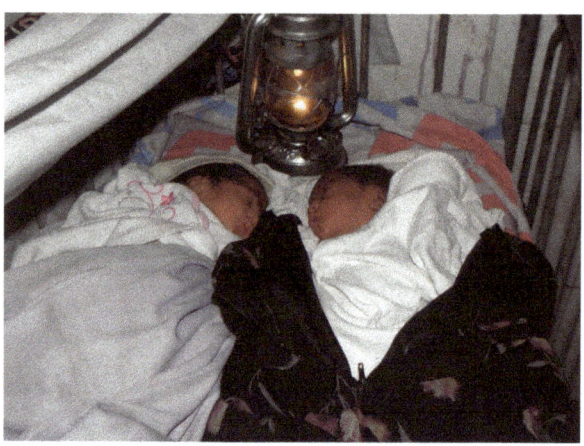
Premature twins born at Mpasa hospital. This is their incubator, a kerosene lamp inside with a blanket over the tiny crib (Summer 2010)

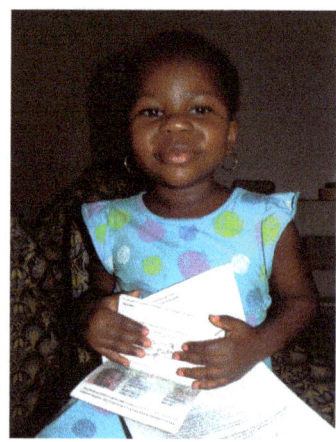
This is the smile of one who has just received her exit visa (Fall 2013)

When Miriam returned for her first visit to Mpasa, she chose to help feed the children instead of eating herself (Summer 2015)

Miriam and her dad (Fall 2020)

Jubilee visiting the babies with Dr. Yohadi (December 2011)

Jubilee organizing a ball game while Miriam stays tightly in her arms (Summer 2010)

Many pirogues parked at the edge of the Congo River in Maluku (Summer 2010)

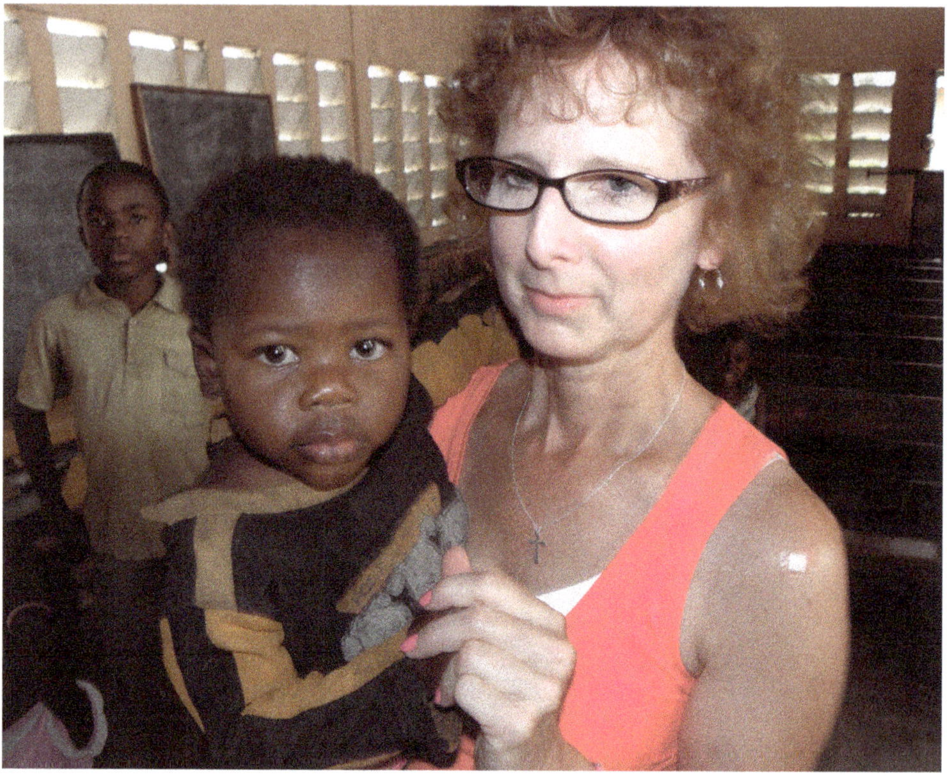

Susie's first day meeting Miriam, before she even knew her name (Summer 2011)

Ed, Miriam, and Susie (Fall 2022)

CHAPTER 13

# Family...A New Definition

*Trust in the Lord with all your heart and lean not
on your own understanding; in all your ways
acknowledge him, and he will make your paths straight.*

PROVERBS 3:5-6

EARLY IN 2012, we started to make plans for a return trip at the end of July. This trip would be extra-special, with my 27-year-old daughter Jaclyn, and another young friend, Emma, 24, planning to join me. Jaclyn felt like Congo was a place she already knew because she had been living it through me and my stories. Emma had been part of our ASP mission trips when she was younger, but now, after completing her nursing degree, she wanted to join us to see what the medical environment would be like in a developing country.

Now that Adolphe and I had become friends, we stayed connected regularly by email. Living in Kinshasa gave him internet access, and his job as our Mission Coordinator afforded him a laptop computer for communication purposes. He called me "his teacher" as our regular communication helped him learn to read and write English with more proficiency. We talked about all kinds of things to give him conversational writing skills. With this, we learned more about each other and our families.

2012 was the year of the General Conference for The United Methodist Church. Because Adolphe understood and spoke English, The Congo Partnership board decided to bring him to the United States to attend the conference and spend some weeks traveling in Delaware and southwestern Pennsylvania. He was asked to visit churches that were current sponsors of our programs and also to create interest for new churches to support us. Ed and I offered our home as his base, and I would visit churches with him when possible, to help with introductions and consistency in presentations. He was with us for seven weeks beginning in late April through May and part of June. He and Ed became close friends and with Jaclyn living nearby, she too was able to get to know him well. This was perfect as we would be traveling there shortly after his departure, giving Jaclyn another reason to feel more comfortable with her decision to go with me.

After his return to Congo, Adolphe sent me an email informing me that Miriam's father had passed away and, in Congo, she would be considered an orphan since her mother had abandoned her at a young age. I had to read it more than once to be sure of what I was seeing. I felt like my heart stopped beating for a few seconds as my breath caught in my throat. A black cloak seemed to have been thrown over me as sadness darkened my thoughts. I walked upstairs to tell Ed this disturbing news. Seeing my eyes filled with tears, he quickly asked me what had happened. I started with these words, "I have just had the worst news ever." Then I proceeded to tell him what I had just learned from Adolphe's email. I told him I was frightened about what would happen to Miriam. I was aware of the state of the orphanages in Congo and was afraid for her. I also understood that it might prove to be impossible for me to see her again.

He stood quietly for a moment and then gently said, "You need to bring her home." Stunned by the suggestion, I stared at him in amazement. Immediately I was filled with doubt at that possibility. My thoughts were jumbled with many doubts: what about our age; what about taking her from her country; was adoption even something Congo was in favor of—especially for white Americans? I pushed aside the idea as being a total impossibility.

Tracking Miriam's situation through Adolphe, I knew she remained in her little green tar paper house. Shako's mother came back there temporarily to care for them both until other plans were made for Miriam. Shako would move to live with his mother.

Our plans were finalized for our trip. I was genuinely excited to be returning, but there was this sadness that lingered over my excitement. Once on the plane with the girls, their joy overflowed into me making us all giddy to arrive. We planned to go directly to Mpasa from the airport. I made this into a tradition from my two previous trips.

Zigzagging through the crazy winding rutted roads on our way to Mpasa was a new experience for the girls that had them sitting at attention as we rocked back and forth in laughter. As we neared the last bend to the center, children were beginning to run toward our car. Their smiles and the calling of my name pulled on my heartstrings reminding me of why I came here.

Miriam's house was just after the bend. I looked over and saw her sitting with many people outside. I called her name; she looked up and began to cry. Shako picked her up and began walking with her in his arms to me. By then, the three of us were standing outside the car. She was still sobbing when he put her in my arms. Her sobbing immediately stopped as she nestled into her favorite position in my arms. I looked at Jaclyn and with tears in her eyes, she said, "Mom, you have to bring her home. She loves you so much." Jaclyn was not one to tear up easily, so I knew her words came straight from her heart.

We stayed awhile at the center visiting with Dr. Yohadi and the medical staff who still lingered there. As it was a Saturday and later in the afternoon, some of the nutrition staff were not there. Jaclyn and Emma were introduced and hugged by each one; they were already loved. Some of the children who lived nearby (Shako among them) trickled in behind us, so the girls were having fun playing chasing games in the courtyard. They were so comfortable in this setting that it seemed like they had been here many times before.

Miriam sat contentedly on my lap, but I saw a raw sadness in her eyes, reigniting my sorrow for her and her brother. Once it was time to head to MPH, with reluctance, I gave her to Shako. I asked Adolphe to be sure they understood we would be back. Parting was difficult, but at least for now, I knew we had a couple of weeks to be together.

On our way to MPH, I shared with Adolphe about Ed telling me I needed to bring Miriam home. He felt we needed to adopt her. I asked Adolphe if that was a possibility in Congo. When he heard my question, he said yes. He continued by telling me that it was possible through The United Methodist Church. There was a pastor who had a small orphanage that kept children who had been chosen for adoption. The adoptive parents paid for their child to be cared for until the paperwork was completed. He shed a little light on the idea that the possibility was there.

I was still unsure that God was calling us to do this. I had too many questions rolling around in my head keeping me from believing. I was also afraid my love for Miriam was overshadowing what God might or might not be telling me. All along, Jaclyn had been silently siding with her dad and, upon hearing Adolphe's response, was begging me to pursue it. That evening while at MPH, we decided to call Ed and ask him how serious he was about adopting Miriam. At the guesthouse, using a Congolese cell phone, we called Ed. I told him what Adolphe shared with me about adopting Miriam. I asked him to tell me if he was serious about adoption. Without a second of hesitation, he said yes and quoted the scripture from the first chapter in James that states "we are to care for orphans and widows in their distress." He wanted me to move ahead with what I could while I was here in Congo. He suggested I call our son Jim to be sure he was on board with us.

Jim sealed our covenant with a yes. When I hung up the phone, Jaclyn and I embraced with exuberance and newfound hope.

The next day we worshipped at Adolphe's church. It was a large church with a full band and several choirs. Not only did we enjoy a worship service, but without a closing worship song, a wedding was about to take place. New chairs were placed in front of us for the wedding party, with the ceremony starting immediately after. Interestingly, following the service, even though they did not know us, they wanted wedding pictures taken with the white visitors. So, somewhere our picture hangs with a beautiful Congolese wedding party on a wall in Kinshasa.

Adolphe spoke with the pastor who was handling adoptions. He gave him contact information for the attorney who would be collaborating with us once we made it official. A series of emails were sent back and forth with an appointment for a Skype conversation to happen while I was still in Congo.

On Monday morning. Emma and Jaclyn were anxious to get back to Mpasa to experience what a nutrition day was like. When we arrived, the children had already been gathered into the large room. A loud welcoming roar came as we entered with clapping and hugging from the adults who had not yet met the girls. Such joy filled that space. Soon the children were singing and clapping their favorite song for us. The girls were clapping and smiling bright cheerful smiles, revealing their delight in being a part of this ministry. One of the precious children stood and offered a prayer for the meal and gratefulness for their new friends.

Miriam was in my arms as soon as the feeding was complete. We all headed outside for a round of games. We brought burlap sacks to introduce them to sack racing. Organizing everyone to make two long lines for the racers to compete took lots of instruction from Adolphe. There was just too much excitement mixed with worry for a turn causing some hilarious confusion. But once we were able to demonstrate how the game was played, cooperation reigned as everyone wanted a turn. Laughter was mixed with sweat as the sun beat down unmercifully on us. Being sure everyone had had a turn, we decided we needed to get out of the sun. The children hung with us for a while and then little by little left for home, each still hopping and jumping out of the compound. The heat did not seem to bother them at all!

I had my first of many Skype calls with the attorney, the founder of Our Family in Africa. She had successfully adopted a Congolese child. With the success of her adoption and the great need for other orphaned children to be adopted, she was determined to help other children become a part of loving families. She began working with Pastor Loma, a United Methodist pastor, helping him to set up an orphanage for children who were to be adopted. He became her liaison with the Congolese government. She was pleased to talk with me, telling me our adoption would be easier as I already knew the child and her family and had some familiarity with Congo. She gave me a list of action items that could get the adoption started on the Congolese end. We were on a whole new journey now!

Emma had a chance to be with a birthing mother and to stand in on a surgery. The primitive setting for the surgery shocked her and made her a bit queasy, as only a local anesthetic was used on the patient to open him for surgery, with a stick placed in his mouth to bear down on for pain. This experience set her in motion to join Mercy Ships as a nurse, joining a mission that brings hope to those in need by sending hospital ships filled with volunteer professionals providing life-changing surgeries.

We brought foam visors for everyone to make and wear for sun protection. It was a busy afternoon helping the children choose the color and decorations they wanted, and then fitting the visor to their heads. All available adults joined in to help us and then made one of their own. By the end of the afternoon, everyone was showing off their new creation. Lots of silly pictures were taken as everybody wanted to model and pose.

The days flew by quickly with the girls. They were leaving after eight days while I would be remaining for another week, working with some other Partnership programs and continuing our adoption process.

The Sending Party for the girls was quite different from the first two. This time Bishop Yemba hosted the party at a downtown Japanese restaurant with a smaller, more intimate group.

Many plates of food were brought to the table to be shared. The conversations were much easier as we were sitting among everyone instead of across the room at a separate table. We had the opportunity to talk easily with one another, take pictures and were presented with gifts. At the end of the evening, we left with big smiles and full bellies.

CHAPTER 14

# Reassurance...
# And That Promise

*And God is able to bless you abundantly, so that
in all things at all times, having all that you need,
you will abound in every good work.*

2 CORINTHIANS 9:8

AT THE AIRPORT we were saddened and wished our plans had included a second week for the girls to stay with me in Congo. But jobs at home were waiting and they did not offer the luxury of more vacation time. I was moving from MPH to Dr. Yohadi's as they wanted me to come back to stay with them. Being alone at MPH did not appeal to me, so I was more than grateful for the invitation to be with them again.

For our adoption to proceed, Adolphe told me that the male figures of Miriam's father's family would have the final decision for Miriam's future. I felt nervous about this as I did not know how they would feel about her being taken away to another country. He put the word out through the community that he needed them to come to the Mpasa center to talk about Miriam.

The next morning, I was in a meeting with Adolphe and others for a future Partnership project. When we stepped out of that meeting, we were told that Miriam's uncles were waiting to see me. Sitting on a bench right outside of the room sat three men, all dressed in suit jackets, waiting to talk with me. We turned around and they followed us into the room. We made our introductions and Adolphe carefully explained to them about me and my husband and our wish to adopt Miriam and take her to the USA to be with us. They talked among themselves; then one spoke. He said to me, "We have been waiting for you."

This puzzled me so I looked to Adolphe to ask and interpret an explanation. The man said, "Before Miriam's father passed away, he had hoped you would come, because he wanted you to have her." My eyes widened in surprise while at that moment, a peace was washing over me like a fragrant spring shower. All this time I had been wondering if this adoption idea was something God had planned for us and now, I knew for sure. His assurance to me came from the voice of another.

I thought about Queen Esther, who was afraid to go before the king to save her people. She feared her decision to do so would be life-threatening to her. So, she did nothing, until the words sent from her uncle, Mordecai, gave her the assurance she needed to complete what she was sent to do. He wrote, "And who knows but that you have come to your royal position for such a time as this?" His words gave her direction of what God wanted her to do. How ironic that mine too, came from the words of an uncle.

After my sincere thank you of gratitude to her each of them, and a round of embraces, I left the meeting in a joyful saunter with a chuckle in my conversation with God, "Okay God, just hit me on the side of my head with a baseball bat to get my attention!".

Now I needed to start checking priority items off the list I received from our attorney. Primarily, I wanted to talk with Adolphe and Dr. Yohadi about where Miriam could stay until our adoption was finalized. I had serious concerns about her going to an orphanage. She had experienced enough trauma in her three years of life, so I did not want to add to that if it could be helped.

Now, too, it was important that we started sharing our news with family members and friends so our prayer warriors could start their prayers of support. We knew it would take a village for this to all come together, even while trusting that God's timing is perfect.

Since Jonathan was one of my main supports from my first trip in 2010, matching my deep love for the Congolese people, I wanted to share with him our news. So, he was among the first of my emails.

Jonathan,

*It certainly is always interesting and sometimes overwhelming to see how God is laying out a plan in our lives. I fell in love with this country upon my first arrival in 2010. I hoped that year, when I came home, that I would be given another chance to return. As we know, I have been gifted that more than once! In 2011, little Miriam attached herself to me during my two weeks stay, and I fell in love with her too. Now, we have become like mother and daughter.*

*When I received the news about Miriam's father's death, I was genuinely concerned as to what would happen to her. After hearing the news, I went to tell Ed what had happened. He looked at me and said, "Well then, you will need to bring her home." At that time, I really had not seriously considered it, but upon my arrival here, and seeing how much she needed me to be with her, I called Ed and asked him if he was serious about that statement, he said instantly, "Absolutely." I then met with Miriam's uncles. They told me that they already knew about me. Miriam's father had told them that he hoped I would return before he died to tell me he wanted me to take her. When I heard this, I was quite stunned, but in a way, quite honored that he trusted me in that way. (I met him in December and had given him a photograph album of Miriam and me together. I told him then how much I loved her. He smiled a big smile.)*

*So, we have decided to start the process to adopt her. I met with Pastor Loma-who does the UM adoptions here. I skyped last night with the agency rep. in the US that collaborates with Pastor Loma. She is excited to start this process. With my experiences here in Kinshasa, she thinks I may also be someone that could help them in the future with other adoptions. So, I am asking for your prayers for us as we enter a huge unknown that we feel we are being led into. As long as the door stays open, we will continue the process. I cannot wait to share her with Epworth. She will be such a gift!*

*Feeling blessed!*
*Susie*

His reply after reading my email:

*Wow, wish you could see my tears of joy – for you…for Miriam… for your family and our Epworth family…and I pray, for Miriam's family. You will be in our prayers, Susie. God will no doubt unfold the plan that is to be for all of you/us! Wow, again!!! I am thrilled! Do you want us to put this out to the congregation for prayer now? OR make this a prayer matter for some of us until you are home? I love your statement, "as long as the door stays open, we will continue the process." AMEN!*

Since I was a member of the Congo Partnership Board of Directors, Jonathan felt it important to share our news with them.

## Reassurance...And That Promise

*Greetings to all,*

*As you know, Jaclyn Keefer and Emma Davis are on their way home from their mission at MPASA. It was a wonderful week there with Dr. Yohadi, staff, children and the elderly women who are part of the feeding program. Susie Keefer will remain for the week and work with Dr. Yohadi and Adolphe on numerous projects related to our mission at MPASA.*

*I am sending this email because of the need for your prayers. [Four months] ago, Miriam, one of the children at the MPASA nutrition center, lost her father. It is a long and tragic story about her family but her father, and MPASA, was doing everything possible to provide a home for Miriam until his death. Susie Keefer developed an amazing relationship with Miriam in her previous missions and had a chance to meet Miriam's father when she was there last December. Susie, and her husband Ed, feel called by God to adopt Miriam! This decision has been supported by Dr. Yohadi and Pastor Loma who manages adoptions through the UM Church. They have begun conversation with the agency in the US who works with the Congolese Church.*

*Susie & Ed have asked for prayers as they continue this process. As Susie says, "we will continue the process as long as the door stays open." I have attached a couple of photos of Miriam and Susie for your prayers. Our lives are never the same when touched by the Christ we discover in others!*

With each email sent to family members and friends, a lovely reply followed with words and prayers of support from each. Jonathan spoke with Ed, and they decided to share the news with the Epworth congregation on Sunday morning. He sent this email to me.

*I called Ed to talk with him and how he felt about offering it for prayer when you were not here today, and he was fine to move forward so I will be making this prayer request tomorrow with Miriam's photo! So, feel the love, God's presence and strength flowing to you as we place this in God's hands. My plan is to do it during the offering time – and then place a picture of Miriam on the altar giving her to God and being open to God's plan and will! GOD LOVES YOU AND SO DO WE!*

*Jonathan*

That Sunday morning, during the offering, Jonathan asked Ed to bring Miriam's picture up and lay it on the altar table. They prayed over her and Ed, asking for God's blessings to rain down on us throughout this process and bring Miriam safely home to be with us. The Epworth congregation applauded. That day, we became one big family awaiting her arrival.

DR. YOHADI AND ADOLPHE asked Annie, a good friend, and the administrative assistant at Mpasa, to care for Miriam while the adoption was in process. Annie was one of the nurses present at Miriam's birth, already loving her. I was pleased and reassured to know she would be in good hands. When the time came for me to leave, Miriam would go home with Annie and live with her family. We would send money monthly for her care.

While working on the details of the adoption, I continued to go to the nutrition center to be with the children during their meal and game time. Even Jubilee joined us for an afternoon bringing handmade sock puppets for everyone. When she opened the suitcase, rolled neatly in rows were 250 pairs of googly eyes looking back at her. Everyone was pressing in to receive their puppet. A room packed with arms covered in sock puppets was a remarkable sight. We had the children hold up their puppets while we sang songs together. Such an explosion of movement and laughter filled the room.

On my last day with Miriam, she was sick with malaria causing a high fever and listlessness. She clung to me closer than ever. Her little body was so hot. One of the doctor's at Mpasa gave her a shot of chloroquine phosphate, the medicine they use to counteract malaria, and doused her with buckets of water. She cried and cried. Once she was back in my arms, I held her tightly, and kissed her on the top of her head assuring her that she would be all right. Her sobs subsided as she settled into my chest and fell contentedly asleep.

A short time later, even though Miriam was not feeling well, Adolphe and Dr. Yohadi had to take her to an appointment with the Territory Administrator. Official paperwork on the death of her father, and the Abandonment Form of her birth mother had to be registered. They were the first formal steps taken to start our adoption. Because of Adolphe's excellent English skills and familiarity with all parties involved, he would be the liaison for us and the Congolese adoption officials.

During the time they were gone, a small number of children remained with me. Because there were so few, everyone was able to have a turn with the bubble gun, play with the jump ropes without a long wait, or sit with me as we gestured our conversations, giggling with one another. Verbal communication was limited without Adolphe.

Once they returned, I was able to spend only a short while with Miriam. Much too soon, we loaded into the car with Annie too, to drop her and Miriam off near her home. I held Miriam on my lap. I was not sure that Miriam understood what was happening to her and the changes that were taking place in her life. It worried me that she would be afraid. She had already experienced so many changes. I needed to step out in faith knowing that God would watch over her during this time of waiting.

Our car slowed and stopped near Annie's home. I was still holding Miriam as we stepped out of the car. As soon as Annie reached out to take her, Miriam began crying as she was pulled gently from my arms. She continued sobbing as they began to walk away. My stomach ached, and my legs felt weak with pain striking my chest with every beat of my heart. I had to grasp tightly and remain steady, standing on His promise… "I will never leave you or forsake you."

My focus now was to survive the next few months managing all the required paperwork, adoptive parenting classes, and preparations in our home for our little girl to join our family.

Boarding the plane, the next day, I collapsed with exhaustion into my seat, prayerfully asking for His guidance in all that needed to be accomplished. This was one of those times that I needed to crawl into His lap and weep.

CHAPTER 15

# Hurry Up...And Wait

*Wait for the Lord; be strong and take heart,
and wait for the Lord.*

PSALM 27:14

MY ARRIVAL HOME was filled with joy. Our lives would be on fast forward for the next several months. We were told the process should take about four months. We needed to start at the top of an exceptionally long list and begin searching for all the crucial information for the required documents. Once all our documentation was compiled, the U.S. Embassy in Kinshasa had explicit instructions on how it all would be placed in what became known as "The Binder." This three-ring notebook would contain documents written in both English and French, collaborating closely with our attorney's adoption administrator, Cami, and the court-appointed attorney in Kinshasa. We were reminded, more than once, of the importance of the placement order of the indexes, documents, and photographs. If anything was left out, or not in proper placement, our adoption could be delayed. We had several Skype conferences to review "The Binder."

Our own children were in their twenties now, so going to the four full-day parenting classes caused us to chuckle. Since we only had a short time span to complete them, and no classes were offered in our area at that time, we had to drive ninety minutes on four consecutive Saturdays to complete the classes. To our surprise, we had an excellent experience learning the challenges we might face when raising a child who might have suffered trauma and who needed extra-loving parental support. Our instructor had adopted three foster children of different ages and nationalities, so she spoke from her own personal life experiences and wisdom gained over the years. We remain friends today.

The requirements included a home inspection and several interviews with our adoptive agency representative. This too was another learning experience that helped us to consider things that we may not have thought of on our own. Everything was falling into place.

Thinking that Miriam would be joining us sometime in November, our church family planned a "Welcoming Shower" for her in early December. Even though there was no information on our acceptance as her adoptive parents and no travel date yet in sight, it was decided to have the party as planned. With sweet Miriam in mind, we were showered in little girl gifts that were sure to bring her days and days of smiles.

On December fourth, we received this email from our attorney...

> You and your husband are the legal parents of sweet Myriam! There is a signed adoption decree indicating this. We have received the legal court documents for her case and the English translations as well. WONDERFUL progress!

This exciting news brought us brief relief knowing that we were accepted as her legal parents. With this acceptance, a flurry of activity began for Miriam in Congo. She needed a Child's DRC passport, a DGM (Congolese Government) immigration letter authorizing departure, Family Affairs Office documentation, visa photos, and a Children Medical Exam with vaccinations. So, our dear little one would be shuttled back and forth to many unfamiliar places over the next few weeks. During this process we learned that, in Congo, nothing has priority status. Every step brought with it a long waiting period for progress toward the next step. We kept reminding ourselves that God's timing is always perfect.

Cami amazed us with her efficiency, knowledge, and positivity, even when things were at a standstill. Amid the wondering if it was ever going to happen, she always had a great piece of advice or something to lift our spirits and shine that light of hope. Her guidance came from her own personal experience, because she had adopted two Congolese children and learned how to navigate through the system's red tape.

**Wednesday, December 12, 2012**
After another period of waiting, I sent her this email:

> *Thank you so much for being such a great "guide" tonight! You were very thorough in sharing all the pertinent information, yet the whole time keeping the children the main focus. With all the paperwork and waiting, we could all become negative and regimented, but you keep reminding everyone what that final outcome is—our beautiful children! I am more excited than ever, and I did not know that was possible! Thank you for doing what you do. It is a gift to so many!*

Time ticked on into the new year with no information coming from the U.S. Embassy about Miriam's visa. Finally in late January we received an email that a date had been set for "The Binder" to be brought to the Embassy. In the past, the process had been for the adoptive parent to come to Congo with "The Binder," meet with the Embassy officials, and then the DGM officials with it all being completed in eight to ten days. When all was finalized, the child's visa was granted, allowing him or her to leave the country with the adoptive parent.

Unfortunately for us, a huge change occurred, which may have been why this waiting period was so long. The Embassy was now requiring the adoptive parent to come to Congo with "The Binder" but return home without the child to allow for a more thorough investigation of the child's family, and to be certain the child had been lawfully approved for adoption. This new process added a three- to six-month waiting period for the child's visa to be approved. If your Embassy appointment was scheduled before February 8th, adoptive parents would still follow the previous procedure. But, if the appointment was set after that date, the new practice would apply. Our date was set for February 15th. Like iron sinking deeply into a pool of dark water, our hearts sank with disappointment. The small light that pierced through this darkness was knowing that I would get to be with Miriam in a few weeks.

I was paired to travel with another anxiously awaiting adoptive parent. Kristen and I met for the first time at Dulles Airport in Washington, D.C. When I arrived at the check-in area, I found her on her knees with two opened suitcases, shuffling clothes from one suitcase to another with some scattered on the floor, trying to adjust the weight for her carry-on to her checked bag. Even though this was our first-time meeting, I could sense her exasperation mixed with apprehension. I assured her that if she had to leave something behind, we could share my things. This was her first trip on her own to Congo, so it was a relief for her to travel with someone who could help her navigate the way and share personal experiences about Congo. We connected right away, feeling like we had been long-time friends.

Our travel and lodging were planned for us through our adoption attorney. She arranged for us to stay in a sweet little cottage behind the home of a missionary family. While we were still settling in, we were called to the front gate to find Adolphe arriving by motorcycle followed by a second motorcycle carrying Annie with Miriam nestled between her and the driver. I walked to her and in seconds she was in my arms. This would be our first overnight stay together.

Since our attorney was concerned about flights or travel interruptions that would cause us to miss our appointments, we arrived two days early. So, the next morning I invited Kristen to join me at Mpasa to meet the children and staff and experience the beauty of our ministry. Dr. Yohadi was waiting on the road to Mpasa to ride along with us. Lots of hugs and smiles to be together again. Her contagious loving heart enveloped Kristen in a big hug that made her feel instantly part of our Congo family.

Watching Kristen soaking in such unfamiliar surroundings rekindled inside me the whirl of emotions I experienced during my first visit. Encountering the suffering firsthand was making her realize the significance of her family's adoption of the little boy named JP, who was awaiting her arrival.

Many children were crowded into the compound awaiting our arrival. As the car doors opened and the crush of the children embraced us, elation was bursting through the air. Trying our best to introduce Kristen to the jubilant smiling staff while making our way to the large room was a challenge we adored. Kristen beamed as she scanned the faces of the beautiful children and heard their voices ringing out their daily songs of praise before their meal. She easily connected with the staff and to the children as she served the precious bowls of food. I could see that the beauty of these moments filled her heart.

The children loved introducing Kristen to our games, especially *pso pso, libada,* wanting her to chase them around the circle. So, we spent a long time running, jumping, and laughing. Exhaustion hit when the exuberance of the morning met the hot sun of the afternoon. Soon we were sitting in the shade of the long narrow porch with as many children who could cluster around us as we tried to catch our breath. Too soon, it was time to say goodbye—as always, a difficult time. Today was bittersweet for Kristen as she knew it would most likely be her only visit. She said a tearful goodbye to each of the staff and tenderly reached out to touch each child. This day would be stamped permanently on her heart.

Both our appointments were scheduled for the same time the next morning. Since Miriam was staying with me now, she came along with us. Once we arrived at the Embassy, it looked as though everyone with an appointment for that day was scheduled to arrive at 9 am. The room had only a few empty seats left with a line of people scheduled to enter. The room was stark, long, and narrow with two clear glass sliding windows on the left wall. Behind each window sat an embassy representative showing little to no expression toward the waiting crowd. Slowly, people were being called by name to the first window and then at some point in their conversation stepped to the second window while the next name was called out.

It was overcrowded and hot as the time dragged into the second hour. Miriam had been content to sit quietly on my lap with a few playthings I packed when unexpected big tears started rolling down her cheeks. With our communication limited, I tried to calm her, but nothing seemed to console her. Finally, a man (who must have sensed my worry) came to me and, knowing her language, asked if he could talk with her. He discovered that she was hungry. He stepped out of the room and came back with a little baggie from a street vendor with a treat she seemed to enjoy. My gratitude overflowed. When the second hour ticked into the third, we were finally called to window one. When the gentleman behind the window accepted "The Binder," I felt the relief of a spring shower sprinkling over me. I was finally moving to the next step.

When Kristen left the following day, Miriam and I moved to Dr. Yohadi's to spend a few more days with each other, and the people we loved. Since Adolphe had a computer with some access to the internet and already playing a significant role in our adoption, Miriam would move to be with his family. She knew Adolphe very well and was comfortable being with him. His family was ready and waiting for her to join them. This change would enable us to see each other through Skype as we waited for her visa to be granted.

When I arrived home, Kristen had added a new story to her Blogpost Journal about her family's adoption journey and all they were encountering along the way. She wrote about her trip to Congo ...

*Making Some REALLY Good Lemonade from My Horrible Lemons*

*Honestly, I have been nervous about going on this trip alone to the DRC for several weeks (as we knew it was coming sometime, we just did not know when). Not the small-butterfly feeling in my stomach nervousness, but the waking-up-every-night-full-of-worry variety. Without going into a ton of detail, there were some "normal" precautions we use in travel--going with a buddy, having reliable transportation at the airport, traveling during the day--that appeared, in my limited viewpoint, to be falling apart. This, along with the fact that Philip was not on the invitation letter and could not get a visa even if we could scrape up the money for Philip to travel with me, left me in a bit of irrational panic.*

*Although I can consciously know that fear is not of the Lord, and I can statistically look at how unlikely it would be that anything would happen to me, for nearly a month I could only focus on the dangers involved in such a trip. It did not help that one day--while thinking whether I should write a blog that looks similar to those You Tube goodbyes--I came out of my thoughtful daze to hear John Mayer singing "Say What You Need to Say" on the radio. An omen, I worried. I was literally and ridiculously scared. I did not have the choice of being disobedient and not going; I just prayed and prayed for God to make the situation less overwhelmingly frightening.*

*And he did just that. With the new guidelines from the U.S. Embassy, suddenly I got to travel with two other people, and those nightmares I had created of being the girl in Taken vanished (if you have not seen that movie yet, do not. It makes you have an irrational fear of traveling, as evidenced by the rant above). I met a sweet woman named Susie at the airport in DC, while I was trying to stuff every item of clothing into my checked baggage, unaware that they weighed your carry-on bags and I had about* ten pounds to shed. After assuring me that if my clothes did not make it, I could borrow hers, we got on a plane headed to Ethiopia. I had found the travel buddy I had been praying for (I will introduce my other travel buddy in my next blog entry).

What I did not know is that God would use Susie to give me more than just peace of mind (and a listening ear) when traveling. As we traveled, I learned that, in 2010, Susie had taken a mission trip to the DRC and had fallen in love with a community right outside the city limits. She had traveled back five times over the next two years as a liaison for the Methodist Church whose program in this community feeds the children once a day, offers a clinic, and has built a water well in the area. Susie comes to meet specific needs of the community, to help create vision for its leaders, and to simply bring joy and hope to the kids of this community through a week of fun, games, and stories about God and Jesus. This time, she was making a trip to adopt a little girl who God had beautifully knit into her life through these visits. She graciously offered to take me to the village the day after we arrived. And there, I learned an important lesson.

We veered off the highway and started down sandy, rocky roads. On either side of us were stone "houses", which consisted mostly of a roof and open, crumbling walls. Children were out playing or bathing from a bucket, while women sat watching them. It began quietly. A few children would catch a glimpse of us in the car, a smile would spread across their face, and they would say, with excitement, "Susie!" We kept driving, some people ignoring us, some peering inquisitively into the windows, and some running alongside the car. Finally, we took our last left-hand turn, and in the clearing, saw the great party that had been prepared for her. It did not have food or decorations--only a hundred children jumping, dancing, and screaming, "Mama Susie, Mama Susie, Mama Susie!" over and over again. She opened the car door, and they swarmed her and followed her into the small gathering spot they had, chanting praise of her return.

Susie is not a celebrity, but she sure looked like one that day. While she visited the friends she had made there, I wandered around to look at the center. I watched as men and women, along with Susie, surrounded the well to discuss its repair (she hoped to purchase a new pump during her visit). I got to pray over a man who had received surgery at the clinic by one of the two doctors there. I got to hold hands with a crowd of smiling children who had just finished their meal. I danced and sang and gave more "high-fives" than my palms could manage. I got the special treat of seeing five babies recently born at the clinic. And I got to be there to see the small awe--of overwhelm and surprise and gratitude--that swept over Susie's face when she learned that one of those babies was named Susie.

I was reminded of the verse in I Thessalonians 4:11: "Make it your ambition to lead a quiet life and attend to your own business and work with your hands... so that you will behave properly toward outsiders and not be in any need." God was using a special-education teacher from a small town in Delaware to carry out His purpose in this otherwise forgotten community. No one would ever know the fanfare that surrounded her visit, but I am sure the Creator of the universe, who had tugged her heartstrings to know and love these people, knew. What I saw that day was nothing short of miraculous: a community brought back to life by the care and concern and obedience of a woman whose ambition was to serve the hungry, and thirsty, and naked, and in doing so, serve her King.

I understood now that God had truly placed Kristen and me together for His purpose. I knew we would remain friends long after this trip. We had connected through our adoptions, but God connected our hearts for much more.

CHAPTER 16

# Heartbreak...Blessings Overflowing

*Give thanks to the Lord, for he is good; his love endures forever.*
I CHRONICLES 16:34

THE NEXT COUPLE of months dragged by without updates on our investigation. On April 11, our attorney had a slight update, but it did not give us any additional information to settle our anxious hearts. She wrote:

> *The embassy responded as follows today to my recent inquiry regarding status of your respective cases:*

"Bell, Keefer, and Olsen are all pending Investigations. That is all the information I can provide."

Cami (who was included in this email) wrote that she was sorry for this news and understood it to be such a challenging time for us. My reply:

Thanks. I was doing fairly good for a while, but lately, I just really need her! She has been asking when her Mama Susie is coming back to get her!

Cami was our best cheerleader, always keeping an optimistic outlook as she sweetly answered:

Oh, it is heartbreaking. I am terribly sorry. If there is anything positive to say about this long, crummy wait... I think it is truly beautiful how she is longing for you.

My response:

It has been the biggest blessing having her with Adolphe and his family. His wife Gina said that they are just "Mary and Joseph" for Miriam because she knows who her mother is and is waiting for her. That was such a neat analogy and made me smile!

More days and months passed without any viable updates as to when her visa would be granted. My hope was to remain content and believing God's hand was in this, but I was faltering. As the days and months kept going by with no official news, it became increasingly difficult for me to keep trusting. Late in August as we were preparing for our son's wedding day (which Miriam was to be part of), I felt His presence. It was just a gentle voice—a whisper in my ear that said, "I know this is a difficult time for you, but I know what I am doing. Just trust me." In that moment a calming reassurance washed over me.

At last, on September 16, almost exactly seven months from our February appointment, we received this email from the Kinshasa Adoptions (U.S. Embassy):

The consul has issued an IR4 visa.
I am writing to inform you that Myriam's visa is issued: Congrat-

*ulations!!! Please have your agency send a lawyer or representative to pick up Myriam's visa tomorrow Tuesday, September 17, 2013.*

We were over the moon with excitement as our minds began to plan. A flurry of instructions from our attorney, spelling out what needed to be done prior to our departure, started to fill my email inbox. A bit of our bubble burst with another challenge set before us. The DRC government issued a new proclamation to all adoptive parents; both parents had to come to the DRC to pick up their adopted child. For us, it meant a second plane ticket, a quick turnaround for required vaccinations, coverage at work in Ed's absence, and additional invitational documents for him to enter the country. We were on a fast track, pulling everything together to leave as soon as possible.

On September 23rd, with our bags in hand, accompanied with huge sighs of relief and hearts filled to the brim with joy, we departed, starting a new leg in our life journey—bringing our daughter home. Our first flight was twelve hours long, with a layover in Ethiopia for a plane change to take us on to Kinshasa for the last four hours. Upon our arrival, Adolphe met us at the airport with a big surprise. Miriam was asleep in his truck with his driver Hugues, waiting for us to arrive. Even though Ed had seen and talked with Miriam on Skype, this would be their first in-person meeting. When we peeked in the truck window, we saw she was fast asleep. Sliding carefully onto the seat, I gently picked her up and caressed her closely to my chest. Her eyes slowly blinked open and seeing who it was, a grand reunion of joyful bliss followed. I introduced her to Ed, and she immediately held out her arms for him to take her. They seemed like old buddies. At that moment, I felt my heart grow three sizes.

Dr. Yohadi and her family were awaiting our arrival with arms opened wide to welcome Ed into the folds of their love. The evening was filled with conversation, mixed with the planning of our next couple of days of appointments to finalize our adoption. Later, while sitting outside, Miriam was hanging onto the back of Ed's neck while he sat on the tailgate of the truck. Precious connections were being made before my eyes.

Our appointment with the DGM (Direction General of Migration under the Ministry of the Interior and Security) was scheduled for Wednesday, September 25th. Prior to that meeting, we needed to prepare all official government documents with Pastor Loma. Each of these documents required a Bordeaux Stamp, proving it to be an authenticated copy. Once we acquired all the stamps, Miriam's exit letter would be granted. For the DGM meeting, we were crowded into a hot tiny room inside the DGM building with Pastor Loma and the officer who would give us the final stamp. There were too many desks crammed into the small space with no seating available for visitors, so we awkwardly stood near his desk as Pastor Loma translated the officer's questions. Thankfully, we left with the final stamp and the promise of receiving the exit visa soon.

An early morning phone call from Pastor Loma the next day added another shock and delay. The Congolese government announced that no adoptive parents could leave the country with their adoptive child. No exit letters would be granted. We were stunned and confused as to what that meant for us since our case had been fully finalized. At first, we thought it might mean a few extra days of waiting before we could leave. But over the next several days Pastor Loma would continue to call with the same message…nothing had changed.

With these additional days of waiting, we chose to spend our time at Mpasa acquainting Ed with the programs I loved so much and where Miriam's life began. To our surprise, Dr. Yohadi had planned a welcoming party for us. A small parade of children presented us with fresh flowers woven with palm leaves that formed a halo around them. We were surrounded by many Mpasa onlookers including the cheerful staff and dozens of familiar children. Everyone wanted to greet Ed and give plenty of hugs to Miriam and me. Our parade grew much larger as we marched up to the big room for the daily meal. Ed was mesmerized by the joyous singing and the well-rehearsed feeding of the children. Miriam easily reacquainted herself with her dining buddies whom she had not seen since moving to Adolphe's home. She laughed and talked and was completely at home in this familiar place.

Dr. Yohadi and Adolphe took Ed on a tour of the facility, sharing with him some major problems with the newly drilled well with an electric pump. Since we were not yet given a date of departure, Ed intended to make good use of his time by working on repairs to the well. During his tour he also noticed some extremely dangerous electrical cables hanging down the wall in the room where the children were fed. He said that needed immediate attention for the safety of the children. After talking with Adolphe, he located the perfect electrician for the job. He was available and able to come the next day to evaluate our needs. He set to work on getting a list for Ed to purchase the necessary parts. God was truly at work through Ed, who was so willing to dedicate his time and money to create a safer, healthier environment for the Mpasa ministries.

Each morning we awoke with hopeful hearts for an optimistic update from Pastor Loma, but the report remained the same—nothing changed. After eight days with no change in sight, Ed had to return home to work. That too was a process, as when we arrived, our passports were held by the DGM until our departure date was set. Pastor Loma graciously helped make the arrangements for us, and soon after, Ed was able to get a flight home. I would remain with Miriam until her exit letter was granted. We felt sure, or at least hoped, that it would happen in the next few days. Dr. Yohadi's family was taking exceptional care of us, and were not ready for us to leave, so their home became ours. Miriam was already calling Dr. Yohadi's mother Koko, meaning grandmother in Lingala.

Miriam felt perfectly at home with Dr. Yohadi's family. She bonded with Koko and the two of them spent many hours in the kitchen area preparing the meals together. At only four years old, Miriam was quite good using knives to chop vegetables, stirring rice over the fire, and pounding the cassava in preparation for cooking. I was amazed at this tiny girl and her efficiency as a cook.

She loved to play dress-up in my clothes and Dr. Yohadi's shoes. We all laughed at her antics in the evenings, dancing in those oversized shoes while swinging her hips to the music with my rolled-up skirt swaying along with her.

It became a joke to us each day that we made the trip or Pastor Loma called that the DGM officer would tell us "Tomorrow". Twenty-nine days of tomorrows had passed. At last, Pastor Loma had a sliver of good news. He had spoken with the American Ambassador and learned that he had been unaware that I was still there waiting for Miriam's exit letter. He seemed to be shocked by this information. He told him Miriam's exit letter would be signed "today". We rejoiced at this news hoping that his influence would help us to hear something from DGM rather than the promise of "tomorrow".

October 22, 2013

In an email to our attorney and Cami, I wrote:

*Pastor Loma was explaining to me last evening that the American Ambassador called him yesterday asking the names of the families still here. He was shocked to find that I was still here after 4 weeks. Miriam's visa is to be signed today. We already spoke about my visa; he was going to look at it this morning and call me if I needed the extension. We are hoping I can leave on Thursday. Let's hope this all really happens today as promised!*

Cami's reply:

*YES, we will hope and pray for the exit letter to be signed today! As soon as it's in your hand, you can go to the airline office to purchase the flight for Myriam and to make the change to your itinerary as well. As long as you have the exit letter in hand, you can schedule the next available flight out. Make certain that Myriam's ticket is purchased in the exact name as her passport - her airline ticket a match the passport. Also, make a few copies of that exit letter, and add one copy to the "DGM at Airport" packet as well.*

*Thanks for the update, we are all thinking of you and praying for you and Myriam to join the rest of your family back home.*

Two more days lumbered by. On the third day, I finally received the email we had been waiting for.

*Friday, October 25, 2013*

*From the U.S Department of State:*

*The U.S. Department of State is reaching out to you regarding your adoption of Myriam Ongenda Earl from the Democratic Republic of the Congo. As noted in the Department's October 23 adoption alert, the Congolese immigration authorities (DGM) provided the U.S. Embassy in Kinshasa with a list of those adoption cases that were approved by the Ministry of Gender and Family and will be able to obtain exit permits to depart the country. We are contacting you to confirm that Myriam Ongenda Earl is on the DGM's list.*

*As Myriam Ongenda Earl has already received a U.S. immigrant visa, you will be able to apply (in person) to the DGM's Administrative Secretary for the exit permit. There is no fee for the service, and the DGM usually takes a minimum of seven days to process each request for an exit permit.*

Because my passport had been held by the DGM, I was not aware that my own visa had run out. Now, I needed to apply for an extension of my visa. Later that day, I learned from the DGM that for me to receive the extension on my visa, I would need additional pages added to my passport as it requires two blank pages and I had just one left. I made the call to the American Embassy only to find out that they close at 12:30 on Fridays. My email arrived after that time, which meant I had to wait until Monday to have an answer. The days of waiting were stacking up and weighing me down.

In my frustration, I sent this email to my prayer friends at home:

*Can you believe that today they issued Miriam's exit letter (Big Hurray!) BUT, my passport has not enough pages left to stamp* my visa (of which I had to pay for an extension, since my 30 day visa here had expired) So, about 2:00 this afternoon, I received a call telling me this information and that I would need to go to the US Embassy and ask for additional pages for my passport or a new passport-they close at 12:30 on Fridays! So now, I can't leave tomorrow or Sunday, as I thought, but will be here until at least Tuesday depending on the speed of the passport problem! God is really pushing me hard!!

Putting more thought into my dilemma, I decided to seek help from the American Consulate with my need for additional pages.

Dear ACS Services and Vice Consul Winkelman:

I am pleased to inform you my Congolese daughter, Myriam Keefer, just received her exit letter from DGM on Friday, October 25, 2013.

Case Number: KIN2013515008
Family: KEEFER
Child: EARL, MYRIAM, ONGENDA

As you are probably aware, I arrived in Kinshasa September 24, shortly after the US embassy issued my daughter's visa to travel to the United States. My husband returned to the United States, but I have been in Kinshasa since September 24th waiting for the exit letter. My new challenge is that my DRC visa expired on Friday, October 25. The DGM was prepared to issue a new visa, but my passport does not have additional blank pages and requested more pages.

The DGM has had possession of my passport all this time, otherwise I would have made my request to you much earlier had I known I was going to be here this long. I have filled out the DS-4085. I understand the petition for additional pages can take several days, but I would respectfully request your assistance in expediting my request, particularly because I have run out of funds to remain in Kinshasa. I am certain you can also sympathize with the stress of waiting for our daughter's DGM exit letter. Can

*I please arrive on Monday morning at the embassy with my old passport, the DS-4085, and fee?*
   *Thank you for your consideration.*

I received this reply:

*Monday, October 28, 2013*

*Hi Karen, [the author's given name]*

*Would you please stop by the consular section today before 1:00 p.m. for that service.*

*Thanks,*

*U.S. Embassy*
*Consular Section*
*ACS Service*
*Kinshasa, DRC*

It was such a relief to read this email. We immediately piled into the car to arrive there before 1:00.

*Tuesday, October 29, 2013*

*From Kinshasa Adoptions (U.S. Embassy):*

*Dear Congo Adoption Agency and/or Adoptive Parent:*

*This email is intended for all adoption agencies that operate in the Democratic Republic of Congo (DRC) and parents who are currently adopting in the Congo.*
   *I would like to address two issues that have been repeatedly raised in recent days by agencies and parents considering Congolese immigration's (DGM) suspension of the issuance of exit permits.*
   *Reissuing visas. If an immigrant visa expires before it can be used, we can issue a replacement visa, BUT the petitioner must*

pay the IV processing fee again ($230) and the medical exams must be redone. We realize it may seem unfair that you must pay again when you could not use the visa for reasons beyond your control. However, the Immigration and Nationality Act specifically states that the fee must be repaid if a new visa is issued after the original expires.

Exit Permits for Children Whose Adoption Was Approved on Or Before September 25th: As we stated in our Adoption Alert, the Congolese immigration authorities (DGM) has told us in writing that, notwithstanding the suspension, they will issue exit permits for children whose adoptions were approved by the Minister of Gender's Interministerial Committee on Adoptions on or before September 25, 2013. The evidence of such approval is the date of the Minister of Gender's stamp on the bordereau for each adoption case. DGM provided us with a list that, according to them, listed all children in this category.

Pastor Loma called early in the morning on Wednesday, October 30th to tell us Miriam's exit visa would be granted today. Adolphe, Miriam, and I sat in the small, stifling hot waiting room at the DGM. Other adoptive parents waited alongside us with the same anxious spirit. None of us felt sure that this day would bring what we all were so desperately hoping for.

Hours later, Pastor Loma appeared in front of me with a huge smile on his face. In his hand was the once elusive exit letter. No words could describe how I felt at that moment. All the days of waiting seemed to fade away, replaced with an overwhelming joy deep in my soul.

Once outside, we were able to allow that joy to explode. But only briefly, as we had a short period of time to take care of our flights and to prepare the paperwork for our departure. While we were checking off things that needed to be done, Pastor Loma made the call to our attorney. By the time we were back to the doctor's house, an email was already in my inbox.

*I understand you have everything, and you are coming home! Tell us the flight!*

I quickly answered as my fingers danced across my keyboard.

*Yes!! It was a moment of joyful tears when I saw the papers! I was also aware that two other families sat by Pastor Loma hoping for some news soon, so I held in my joy until I was away from there.*

*Our flight is tomorrow at 12:40. We are meeting Pastor Loma at 7:30 to go through the final stage at the airport. Flight #831V, then #500V arriving at Dulles at 8:30am on Friday.*

*Lots to share with you when I get home!*

*Thank you again for your prayers and constant support!*

Then from Cami:

*Sue, a couple final things...*

*Do you have your "DGM at AIRPORT" packet? You need to ADD a copy of the DGM exit letter to the packet.*

*If the DGM officials at the airport want to see your original documents, make sure you get them back. You cannot get new originals if they are lost. They should only keep the copies in your "DGM at AIRPORT" packet.*

*Did you pay Master Okoko his legal fee?*

*Did you pay Pastor Loma his fee?*

*Please try to settle any fees owed before you leave or make arrangements for a bank wire to them. Ask them for a receipt and write one up if you do not have one for them to sign.*

*I assume Dr. Yahadi will arrange getting you to the airport but let me know if I can do anything to help from here.*

*Pastor Loma may suggest that you hire someone to escort you through the process at the airport, as it is much more complicated when you are departing with a Congolese child and must prove your adoption at several checkpoints. Some families have received help from Jeffrey Travels, but there is also an agent that Pastor Loma knows, and he may ask for him to help you. Families have paid him between $20 - $40 in the past. If so, confirm the amount up front, and pay him discreetly at the end, before you go into the large waiting area.*

We arrived at the airport the next morning with all the critical items checked off my list. I felt the rapid flutter of my heart, knowing we were on our way home.

Tiny, yet so determined, Miriam insisted on pulling her own little suitcase through the parking lot. As we followed behind Pastor Loma, he effortlessly orchestrated all that needed attention prior to our departure. We said our goodbyes to him with gratefulness for his tireless work guiding us through the seemingly endless days of waiting.

Adolphe stayed with us until we had to move to the "passengers only" side. It was a bittersweet goodbye as he had dedicated most every day to being with us, helping me to converse with the doctor's family and driving us each time to the DGM. Since his family had been Miriam's caregivers for the past seven months, she had become a part of their family, so even though he was overjoyed by her adoption, he was feeling a bit blue.

I was anxious about the long flight, worrying that she might be afraid or cry, but she showed no signs of either as she nestled into her seat staring out the plane window while enjoying a snack the airline attendant had given her. She slept many of the hours we were on the plane, each time awaking with no signs of fear or anxiety. Almost 24 hours later, on November 1st, we landed in Washington D.C. When I realized I was back on U.S. soil, relief wrapped around me like a warm blanket.

That comfort got us through customs and baggage pick up. As we entered the waiting area, I scanned the crowd, finding Ed standing there grinning from ear to ear. Somehow that made all the days of endless trials begin to fade, being replaced with incredible joy. We were home. The Master Weaver was creating new vivid colors with rich depth to our tapestries.

CHAPTER 17

# Questions...Answers

*And my God will meet all your needs according to the riches of his glory in Christ Jesus.*

PHILIPPIANS 4:19

ALL THE DAYS and months we spent waiting during our adoption process have puzzled me as to what God's purpose was. I believe God's timing to be perfect even though my timetable and His are most never the same. I am a planner and like to know ahead of time what and how to be prepared. But the four months that turned into fourteen, and the $5,000 to $22,000, left me with question marks galore and no planning calendar.

As I mentioned in an earlier chapter, the adoption period was to be about four months. We were prepared for that and possibly a month or two longer, but not ten months. We also felt we could afford $5,000 as the quoted cost, and maybe a bit more, but not four times more.

In an article about waiting, Ruth Clemence writes:

> We spend a lot of our time waiting. Waiting in line. Waiting for news. Waiting for a response. Waiting for a promotion. Waiting for the next season of life. God is at work in our waiting. We might not see any changes in these times of waiting, particularly through times of difficulty and periods of personal growth, but there is a plan and purpose in all of it.
>
> God can see things that need to be ironed out in our hearts and our lives that would only remain creased and messy if it wasn't for the refining times of waiting.

There are many Biblical characters whose lives were groomed and reshaped through waiting. Abraham was one who was promised an heir through his wife Sarah despite her old age. Their waiting period lasted twenty-five years. Sarah eventually gave birth to Isaac, "and the Lord did to Sarah as he had promised" (Genesis 21:1). But I wondered what God's purpose for our waiting was.

During the extended period of time that I spent waiting in Congo, I continued to go to Mpasa with Dr. Yohadi most every day. More and more people recognized me and knew me by name. I became a trusted mindeli (white person) among them. I fed their children. I was available to play, hold, and even walk home with them. The familiarity and trust I garnered was part of God's reshaping and grooming process for me.

When Miriam and I returned home late to Dr. Yohadi's our last evening in Congo, she was waiting to share something with me. She told me that while she was at Mpasa, three women had walked five kilometers looking for me. They said to Dr. Yohadi, "We are looking for your Susie. We understand she feeds your children here and our children are starving. Can she come to feed our children?" When she finished her story, I sat stunned. Knowing I was leaving early the next morning, it weighed heavily on my mind. My heart ached as I thought about those mothers, their starving children, and their plea for me to come and feed them.

Throughout my flight, my mind kept wandering back to those mothers and the desperation they felt. Once home, I shared their story with Ed. We had sponsored children through worldwide organizations for many years but were disenchanted to find out that only a small portion of our pledge money was used for the children while the rest was used for administrative costs (mostly large salaries). Ed weighed the idea for a while and thought that if we could assure sponsors that their donations would be used for feeding the children, with no portion used for administrative costs, maybe we could open a nutrition program in that area.

We began to share our proposal with family and friends, finding positive responses, with some offering helpful suggestions as we began to put together a plan. Prayerfully we started to research the possibilities. We turned to Adolphe and Dr. Yohadi for guidance on how we could make this dream become a reality.

Over the next several months, as things began to fall into place, we knew that God was at work guiding and giving us direction. Dr. Yohadi's mother owned a piece of land in the area where the women lived. She was willing to lease the land to us for a small fee. We worked together with Bishop Yemba and the United Methodist Episcopal Area with government regulations on nutritional programs. Dr. Yohadi and Adolphe worked with a local builder to quote the cost of constructing a building that would house the feeding of the children. The leased property already had two small buildings that could be used for supplies and the cooking area could be added to the back of one of those buildings.

As things started to progress, we realized this budding ministry needed a name. Ed wanted the name to honor Miriam, so we asked our friends and family for help. After several ideas were shared with us, our friend Phil called with a brilliant idea. He said because we were inviting children to come and be fed, maybe we should call it Miriam's Table. Knowing Miriam had been fed at a nutrition center, he said now she could be the one feeding others. Instantly, smiles bloomed across our faces as we knew that was the perfect name.

Once Miriam arrived, we planned a legal USA adoption. This would assure her U.S. citizenship bearing an American passport, which would be important for her when we returned to Congo. It was finalized and celebrated in May of 2014, so now we were comfortable with her accompanying me back to Congo without a problem.

With summer quickly approaching, and Miriam's Table continuing to become a reality, I needed to return to tie up any loose ends for our proposed opening in the fall. This time we would be staying with Adolphe's family because they considered Miriam part of their family and were insistent, we stayed with them. Our arrival was quite a reunion for both Miriam and Adolphe's family. They enveloped me in their love as well, making me feel like part of the family, too.

Miriam's Table is located in an area known in the Mpasa Region as the "poorest of the poor". It is set back where the travel is a bit more rugged than where we travel to feed the children at the Mpasa Nutrition Center. It is a very sandy area down a hill near a small river, and is only accessed via a four-wheel drive vehicle, a motorcycle, or on foot. Adolphe's vehicle had four-wheel drive, so we were able to inch our way down the tricky path-like road.

It was an exciting moment for me when I saw our building beginning to take shape. Each block was made by hand using sand, cement mix, and mud, carefully molded into a metal mold, then shaken out to dry in the sun. It was like watching someone at the beach flip a sandcastle mold upside down and carefully pull up on the mold to form a perfect sandcastle. Hundreds of bricks that had been made one by one were lined up drying in the sun.

Dr. Yohadi, Adolphe and I met to select a staff and a director, and to create a list of essential items we needed to purchase to be ready for the opening. We put together a team that we agreed would be perfect for the needs of the program. Adolphe and I went to a wood shop to order benches for the adults who would be feeding the smaller children to sit on, and tables for serving. I was in awe watching the woodworkers using hand tools to cut and plane the wood into perfectly smooth finishes. They were true craftsmen.

The next day, several of us went into downtown Kinshasa to purchase cooking and feeding equipment and large water barrels to carry fresh water for cooking. We also went to a large warehouse to order large sacks of grains, sugar, and other porridge ingredients to create the mixture that provides enough vitamins and minerals for a full day's nutrition, as it may be the only meal, they receive each day. The minister of health committee created the recipe for all nutrition programs.

Miriam was content to spend some time with her little friends at the Mpasa Medical/Nutrition Center. She played games and ran and laughed but told them that now she only spoke English. The staff at Mpasa missed her and were delighted to see her again. We all talked and laughed together, too. Always so much joy among us.

Our days flew by spending hours each day planning, preparing, checking, and rechecking our lists while keeping an eye on the builders. Each time we visited, more inquisitive people came by to see who we were (especially the white lady) and what we were doing. The word about a nutrition program coming to this area piqued interest around the surrounding community.

Prior to my leaving, Dr. Yohadi called the newly chosen nutrition team together to have our first meeting of introductions, share our vision for the ministry, our expectations for them as a team, and how and when the program was to begin. I gifted each of them a Miriam's Table apron that my sister made. They were received with gratitude and pride to be part of this brand-new ministry.

Standing here, with this team beaming with pride, surrounded by the partially built walls and drying bricks, I knew why God needed fourteen months of waiting with the additional thirty-seven days in Congo for me. It was for this moment: the birth of Miriam's Table.

Only the Master Weaver knew about this moment. He was weaving it with a bright splash of color knowing it was a moment that would change our lives completely.

And that it has.

CHAPTER 18

# Faith Is a Noun... Trust Is a Verb

*Trust in the Lord with all your heart
and lean not on your own understanding;
in all your ways submit to him,
and he will make your paths straight*

PROVERBS 3:5-6

WITH PREPARATIONS FOR our ninth ASP trip nearly complete and just three weeks until departure, two of my adult leaders and five of our youth canceled. It was too late for me to make changes with the ASP administration, so we would still need to pay for those slots and be short leadership. I was heartbroken, worried, and upset by this last-minute discouraging situation. Each year I always planned everything to be in perfect order with the teams, the van rental for travel, and necessary paperwork prior to our departure. Now, what was I to do? I was able to ask my two brothers-in-law to step in as team leaders, but too late for additional youth to be added.

To my surprise, the week ended up being "the best ever" as usual, but during that week, God spoke very clearly to me. He said, 'This is not your mission trip. It is mine and I will bring the people whom I want to make up the teams." All these years, I had been taking possession of these trips. God was patient with me in allowing me to be blessed each year, even though I was taking credit for the success of that trip due to my "perfect planning." It was not until this trip that He taught me what I should have known all along: it was His mission, not mine. For the next eight years, I never worried again. I allowed God to be my guide and choose whom He knew needed to be there.

So, when we started to plan the ministry of Miriam's Table, from the earliest moments, He clearly told me that Miriam's Table was His and that He would be our guide. I did not need to worry as He "had this!". Each time I would get a little nervous about having the funding needed for our budget, I would receive in the mail what I called a "random check"—an unexpected donation. I knew then that God was tapping me on the shoulder to tell me once again He was in charge.

The doors of Miriam's Table opened on October 13, 2014. According to the figures given to us, we planned to feed about 150 children each day. On day one, we had 65 beautiful children, frightened but hungry. After studying the photographs sent to me, my mind recalled those magazine pictures I had seen many years ago. Staring back at me were sets of big brown eyes on tremulous faces, some tear-stained, with sticklike arms and basketball-sized bellies. In that moment, I knew how vital this ministry was.

Within a few days more children began to come as parents learned from others that the meal was free. Within two weeks, our numbers were at 250. We were able to feed that number but did not have funds to feed more. We knew that there were at least another 100 children needing to be fed.

We also knew the importance of fresh water and had planned our budget to include the purchase of fresh water for cooking and cleaning. Waterborne diseases are a constant threat to the lives of children. We wanted to figure out a way to bring a fresh water well to Miriam's Table.

Unbeknownst to me, God already had a plan in motion. In the spring of 2015, our friend Phil asked me if I could come and share Miriam's Table with his Rotarian club. I was unaware of what Rotary was or that they are a dedicated service organization to improve lives in communities around the world hoping to create lasting change.

Thanks to Phil's invitation, I had the privilege of speaking to the Rehoboth Sunrise Club in Rehoboth Beach, Delaware, sharing with them our Miriam's Table ministry and our vision for the future. The last slide of the presentation presented our vision.

1. To have the funds to be able to feed the 100 waiting children.
2. To have a fresh water well that would serve not only Miriam's Table, but the surrounding community.

I had no idea that they funded such projects, but within minutes after we adjourned, I had been promised the money to feed the children for a year, and informed that a grant was available for freshwater wells through Rotary International.

The grant process was an intense process, but in early 2017, a freshwater well was dug at Miriam's Table, providing fresh drinking and cooking water not only for Miriam's Table, but for the surrounding community. What a glorious time that was. The pictures shared with me were filled with smiling faces while cupping their hands to drink the fresh, clean water.

EACH YEAR, MIRIAM AND I travel to Congo to spend time at Miriam's Table. My heart soars as I watch Miriam handing bowls to the children. Her life has come full circle. As she was once fed by others, now she is feeding others. As she is now a teenager, she loves to pick up the smaller children and hold them in her lap, spooning the food into their open mouths exactly as she remembers I did with her.

We feed about 350 children daily with a dedicated staff of eleven. They work tirelessly each day making sure that every child is fed. I always remind them that they are the hands and feet of Christ—missionaries in their own country.

Now we see children running, jumping, and playing, with huge smiles replacing the sad hungry faces with little energy to play that we used to see. They especially love when we visit as we spend hours playing all their favorite games. They continue to roar with laughter at duck, duck, goose, chasing each other as fast as they can. Parachute games, jumping rope, blowing bubbles, and sack races are also among the favorites.

The future of Miriam's Table looks bright as we know God has more plans for us. With eyes and ears open and hearts afire, we await His guidance.

When I stepped off that plane for the first time in August of 2010, I never imagined what God had prepared for me. The Democratic Republic of the Congo defines who I am today. That touch from a tiny little girl reached deep into my heart tied right to my soul… transforming me forever. The Master Weaver continues weaving a magnificent tapestry for me.

# Afterword

## *Miriam Oleka Keefer*

WHEN MY MOM began to write this book about our story, I wasn't so sure about it all until she asked me to read it. I still wasn't very sure how I felt about it one bit.

Then I was asked to lunch with the publisher, and he asked me if I would write something for the end of the book? And still I wasn't so sure until my mom said maybe I could think about it as a birthday gift to her. Soon after, I began to read the book and finished it fairly quickly. When I was reading the book, it brought tears to my eyes as everything flooded back to me. When I first held my arms out for my mom to pick me up, and now I truly realize how lucky I am to be so loved by these two people and I truly give thanks to my dad, Ed, who thought of the idea to bring me home.

When I first arrived at my American home, I was nervous when I saw the dog in the house. I was afraid of dogs, but soon she and I would become close friends. I remember how my mom's friend Susie Bond, my new sister Jaclyn and her wife Julie, the dog named Taylor, and Mom all crowded in the bathroom giving me my first bath on American soil. It was my first time ever seeing bubbles and having fresh warm water flowing down over me. My mom says that I sat under the faucet at bath time for several months while the warm water flowed down my back.

When I arrived back in Congo, it had been eight months since I had been adopted and become a U.S. citizen. When my feet touched my homeland soil, I could tell I was home again. It felt so refreshing smelling the Congo air. And when we went back to the nutrition center where I met Mom, do you know what I said? I said "I speak English" to all the kids who tried to talk with me. When my mom began to pass out the bowls of food, I remember deciding to help pass out the bowls to the others, one of the reasons why they named our nutrition center Miriam's Table.

But now, ten years later, I return to Congo every one to two years. I go with my mom and since I'm older now I truly understand the meaning of Miriam's Table and the reason we feed these kids. It brings me happiness to see them run to us when we arrive. They cling to us as we head down to the center. Seeing these kids smile brings happiness to me and everyone around us to see their full stomachs and wide smiles, knowing they finally do have a place where they can eat and thrive.

# Acknowledgments

FIRST AND FOREMOST, to my husband Ed, who has been the wind beneath my wings in all the opportunities, challenges, and endeavors I have taken on. He never wavers in his support, always encouraging me to keep growing. He completes me.

To my children, Jaclyn and Jim, and Miriam for their inspiration to write our story. From the moment Jaclyn and Jim said yes to bringing Miriam into our family, we formed an unbreakable bond of love for which fills my heart to overflowing.

A special *Thank You* to my publisher Ron Sauder, whose first words to me after receiving my manuscript were *"You are a natural born storyteller. It gets off to an irresistible start."* From that moment, his constant encouragement kept me on the path to the completion of this book. I am beyond grateful for his guidance and never-ending support.

To Jack Shitama, for teaching a course for first time authors at Camp Pecometh, Maryland. It was during those two days that I was inspired by Jack to write my story. His step-by-step details of getting from page one to a completed book was the guide I referred to throughout my writing process. As he is an author of several books, his invaluable influence continued as one of our Beta Readers, working with me and my publisher, on our first edit. Camp Pecometh also became my writing inspiration refuge where I spent time on several personal retreats.

To Mary Fleming, Rev. Jack Harnish, Bishop Peggy Johnson, and Michele Stouffer, for being my team of Beta Readers. Each of you were an inspiration to my writing process by sharing your emotional connections to the story and adding suggestions on keeping readers engaged.

To Adolphe Yamba Yamba, whose never-ending smile was the light that shined through the crowd on my very first visit to Congo and has never dimmed. His deep faith has lifted me up over the years allowing me to see beauty in everything God brings my way. His family welcomed Miriam into their home, quickly becoming a member of their family over the months they cared for her. They extended that love for her to me, continuing to open their home to us each time we return to Congo.

To my dear Congolese friend, Dr. Rebecca Yohadi, whose outstretched arms welcomed me many times into her home, giving me a place to live surrounded with the love of her big extended family. Even when Miriam and I were there for 37 days, they never tired of caring for us. Tears fell when we received her exit visa as we had become part of her family.

To Jonathan Baker, who shares in leaving pieces of his heart with the Congolese people. His knowledge and guidance over the years has been invaluable to my personal ministry in Congo. He was key in keeping my spirits up with an email awaiting me most every day, filled with words of encouragement and prayers for our safety while waiting for Miriam's exit visa.

# About the Author

## *Susie Keefer*

AFTER HER FIRST mission trip to the Democratic Republic of the Congo in 2010, Susie Keefer left a piece of her heart with the people there. That piece of her heart grew with the adoption of a Congolese child by Susie and her husband Ed, which in turn inspired the establishment of a nutrition program that honors their daughter. *He Hoped I Would Come* is her story of experiencing God as He unfolds His plan with the utmost of inspiration. A wife and mother of three, Susie loves leading ladies' Bible studies, giving women opportunities to share and grow in faith. She lives in Lewes, Delaware.

For more information on Susie's ongoing work in the Congo, please visit MiriamsTable.org or scan this QR code:

# For Further Reading

THIS BOOK IS my own personal story as I have lived and experienced it, and it requires no written references to read and understand. However, in some places I have cited other authors and publications to provide background or illustrate important points.

Those sources are listed below, organized by chapter, for those who wish to explore further.

### Chapter 1
Corrie Ten Boom with John and Elizabeth Sherrill, *The Hiding Place*. Chosen Books, 1971.

### Chapter 3
Adam Hochschild, *King Leopold's Ghost: A Story of Greed, Terror, and Heroism in Colonial Africa*. Houghton Mifflin, 1998.

COLONIAL GENOCIDE AND THE CONGO - Early Day Motions - UK Parliament. https://edm.parliament.uk/early-day-motion/30788

UN Environmental Programme, Can the Democratic Republic of the Congo's mineral resources provide a pathway to peace? https://www.unep.org/news-and-stories/story/can-democratic-republic-congos-mineral-resources-provide-pathway-peace

Wiese, Bernd Michael, Lemarchand, Ren, Payanzo, Ntsomo and Cordell, Dennis D. "Democratic Republic of the Congo". *Encyclopedia Britannica*, 11 Jan. 2024, https://www.britannica.com/place/Democratic-Republic-of-the-Congo.

**Chapter 6**
Joseph Conrad, *Heart of Darkness*. Edited by Robert Hampson and Owen Knowles, Penguin Classics, 2007.

UN Development Programme, The Magic of Cassava: Adapting to climate change in the Democratic Republic of the Congo. https://undp-climate.exposure.co/the-magic-of-cassava

**Chapter 12**
Amy Carmichael, paraphrased from *If: What Do I Know of Calvary Love* (Christian Literature Crusade, 1938), in Leslie Ludy, *Authentic Beauty: The Shaping of a Set-Apart Young Woman* (Multnomah, 2007), 248.

**Chapter 17**
Ruth Clemence. 7 Encouraging Bible Stories That Prove Waiting Is Worth It. https://www.biblestudytools.com/bible-study/topical-studies/encouraging-bible-stories-that-prove-waiting-is-worth-it.html

www.ingramcontent.com/pod-product-compliance
Lightning Source LLC
Chambersburg PA
CBHW042012060526
44119CB00123B/439/J